SMALL
Groups
in the church

a handbook for creating community

Thomas G. Kirkpatrick

An Alban Institute Publication

The author and the Alban Institute gratefully acknowledge permission to reprint excerpts from

The Different Drum: Community-Making and Peace by M. Scott Peck. Copyright © 1987. M. Scott Peck, M.D., P.C. Reprinted by permission of Simon & Schuster, Inc.

Discussion: A Guide to Effective Practice, 1ˢᵗ Edition, by David Potter and Martin P. Anderson. Copyright © 1963. Reprinted with the permisson of Wadsworth Publishing Company, Inc.

"Fellowship: Key to Witnessing" by Richard Halverson. Reprinted from HIS magaine, December 1967, © InterVarsity Christian Fellowship. Used by permission.

Looking at the Small Church: Frame of Reference by Lyle E. Schaller. Copyright 1977 Christian Century Foundation. Reprinted by permission from the July-August 1977 issue of *The Christian Ministry.*

Making Friends of Enemies. Copyright © 1987 by Jim Forest. Reprinted by permission of The CROSSROAD Publishing Company, New York.

The People Called: The Growth of Community in the Bible by Paul D. Hanson. Copyright © 1986 by Paul D. Hanson. Reprinted by permission of HarperCollins Publishers, Inc.

The Preaching Event by John R. Claypool. Copyright © John R. Claypool. Reprinted by permission of the author.

Sharing Groups in the Church by Robert C. Leslie. Copyright 1970, 1971, by Abingdon Press. Excerpted by permission.

Library of Congress Catalog Card Number 95-75683
ISBN 1-56699-151-X

CONTENTS

ACKNOWLEDGMENTS

I am grateful to colleagues:

Rev. Paul McCann, whose belief in small groups spurred me to commence this project.

Dr. Dick Ferrin, who allowed me time to write the first draft during my teaching tenure at Whitworth College.

Rev. John Pierce, for his constant encouragement to pursue publication.

Rabbi Mordechai Liebling, for introducing me to the Havurot movement.

Rev. Jim McCrea, for his wise journalistic advice and detailed editorial assistance.

Celia Hahn and her Alban editorial team for their support, wisdom, and competence.

I am also grateful for the support and recommendations of the many students and churches who "field-tested" early drafts of my work.

And I am especially grateful to my family for their immeasurable encouragement and support. It is to them that I dedicate this book:

To my wife, Carol, and to my children, Matt, Michele, Chris, and Juliann.

INTRODUCTION

In the 1960s and seventies, "renewal" was high on the agenda of many
of our churches, especially in mainline denominations. What's more, the
development of a sense of community through small groups was a frequently cited panacea for church renewal. But what has happened to this
impulse in our churches? Why haven't more of our churches come alive
through a small-group ministry?

As this book goes to press, Robert Wuthnow's comprehensive
report on the state of the small-group movement, *Sharing the Journey:
Support Groups and America's New Quest for Community*,[1] finds that
40 percent of American adults currently participate in small, diverse
groups that meet regularly and offer care and support. Two-thirds of
these small groups are connected to churches and synagogues. Clearly,
people still seek spiritual renewal and a sense of community through
small groups!

Wuthnow suggests, however, that the small-group movement is at
a crossroad. For all its success in helping millions of us find emotional
and spiritual care and support, the small-group movement faces the challenge of extending care to those beyond the groups, serving the wider
community, and remembering the One who is ultimately responsible for
creating community and nurturing spirituality.

While Wuthnow's report is instructive and his assessment warrants
careful attention, I find yet another crucial factor to consider. A primary
reason renewal has not become *more* of a reality for us is that so few of
our church leaders know how to expand their small-group ministries. In
short, most of our clergy and lay leaders have little training in this dimension of congregational life and mission.

This book is a planning and training handbook for church leaders who desire to discover how Christian community can emerge through small groups. It grows out of my own participation in small groups, my active professional experience in assisting numerous congregations to come alive through their small-group ministries, and my formal academic training.

In fact, my participation in a personal sharing group is *the* single most important experience in my life during the past twenty-five years. Likewise, my regular participation in professional support groups has a vital, integrating impact on my ministry.

Then, too, my service for five years in campus ministry and for eight years as a parish pastor provides valuable insight into how small-group ministries emerge. And my service as a church renewal consultant over the last fifteen years offers a most enriching viewpoint for seeing how numerous churches plan small-group ministries, train small-group leaders, and expand their small groups.

It has also been my privilege to complete two doctoral programs in interpersonal and small group communication. One was a professionally oriented program focused on creating community through relational small groups in the church. The other was academically oriented and focused on leading effective group discussions in small task groups in the church.

Overview of Book

Section 1 sets "The Context." The first chapter provides a new perspective for understanding and experiencing community. Based on this fresh perspective, chapter 2 considers the vital role small groups play in creating Christian community; it offers guidelines and insights for developing community in your church.

Section 2, "The Planning," gives practical suggestions for creating a plan, recruiting potential small-group leaders, and planning a leadership training course.

Section 3, "The Training," presents a detailed training course outline to use with prospective small-group leaders.

Section 4, "The Expansion," helps you interpret and implement what you've read—to begin new small groups.

Welcome to this exciting journey. Our prospect for creating community through small groups has great promise, indeed!

SECTION 1

The Context

CHAPTER 1

The Possibility of Community

The Promise of Community

Imagine with me that it is Sunday night, time for the weekly meeting of a small sharing and support group. With juice or coffee in hand, all six group members have finished their greetings and chitchat. As they settle into comfortable living room chairs, their conversation gets more personal.

Mary says, "You all know that I've been feeling pretty low these last several months. Well, at your urging, I did go to the doctor last week. I discovered that I'm on the verge of clinical depression due to a chemical imbalance. I'm already feeling a lot better, taking some medication. I don't know what would have happened without all of you to talk with."

Ron follows up, "Wow, Mary, I'm so glad you found the courage to get a check-up. I remember last month when Jackson helped you finally admit to yourself how reluctant you are to see a doctor. And it's great that you're beginning to feel better again!

"You know, when you were talking just now I had some insight into how flat my own life is. I think I'm doing okay physically. But I guess I'm not sure that I want to continue in my present line of work. I think I've been where I'm supposed to be these last few years, but I'm coming to see that my blah work life has got to change. My life is probably half over, and I don't want to continue in work I have no passion for. I know a lot of people do, but I don't think I'm willing to go on this way forever."

With Ron's permission, the group sensitively probes for possible underlying reasons for his lack of satisfaction and explores with him some possible alternative work options.

After Greg and Pat tell about fairly routine weeks, it's Brandy's turn. "I don't think I'm in touch with myself lately. I know that my life has become very present-oriented. In fact, everything I do seems centered in the present. I'm usually future oriented; I have plans to look forward to. Being newly married, I'm finding that step-parenting takes a lot of adjusting. Oh, we have some plans for next summer, but nothing sounds very appealing to me."

"I wonder," remarks Greg, "if you're taking good enough care of yourself lately, Brandy. If not, no wonder you can't get a handle on what's happening."

"You mean I don't have enough energy to meet all the demands on my time?" responds Brandy. "Hey, that makes a lot of sense. But you know what? I'm not sure I even know what I'd like to do for myself to get refueled. I really feel stuck."

After the group helps Brandy begin to figure out how to schedule more personally enriching time, Jackson updates the group about a writing project and tells about some exciting summer plans. Then he says, "I want to tell you about how I've been coping with the uncertainty of being transferred. Last year at this time, not knowing if we were going to stay here or move was driving me nuts. Well, two plans I made last fall have helped me a lot. I just finished teaching that new course I've been telling you about, and it really went well. There may even be another book to write based on what I did and learned. Then, too, I've gone ice fishing a lot on my days off this winter. Fishing is my therapy; it helps keep my life in balance. Even if I don't catch anything, it's great just to be outdoors. I even saw an eagle flying overhead this week. So those two plans I made have meant a world of difference—not knowing what the future will bring hasn't even bothered me lately!"

Group members express joy with Jackson at his relief from debilitating uncertainty. They conclude their time together with prayer for one another.

As you can see, these group members feel they can count on one another to listen and care, to provide support and strength. Because confidentiality is a given, members can be vulnerable with one another. Then, too, they can expect to be challenged when appropriate, knowing that everyone is at times prone to self-deception and denial. They rely on each other's prayers, confident that circumstances change for the better as a result of these prayers.

In short, these group members experience an openness to talk about the more important things in their lives. Sufficient freedom to be themselves, without judgment from others, is present because they share their hopes and dreams, failures and feelings, ideas and suggestions. And from such openness and acceptance, including prayer for one another, they experience a powerful kind of bonding or warmth that brings growth and change—a feeling of being rejuvenated, as if they receive new strength and Life![1]

In point of fact, they did! These group members were experiencing the essence of authentic Christian community: sharing their lives with one another and their Lord. This is what *koinonia* is all about. *Koinonia*, the Greek Septuagint and New Testament word for "fellowship," actually means *sharing something with someone*.[2] And these group members were sharing their very lives at a most personal, intimate level.

Most humans yearn for this type of meaningful relationship A basic affirmation of Christian faith is that we are made for relationship with God and one another. I know I feel most alive, most human, when I relate with others at the genuine and "gut" level, reaching beyond phoniness or superficiality. This kind of relationship is deeper than that of acquaintances or even friends. It is marked by the quality of sharing that *good* friends with a *close personal relationship* enjoy—love for one another. This is a relationship characterized by openness, acceptance, warmth, and growth. And it is this very kind of sharing and relating in the church that produces a sense of Christian community.

It is our close personal relationships, our love for one another in the church, then, that offers the promise of Christian community.

The Problem of Community

Our Christian Life together, love for one another among believers in the church, is to be *the* distinguishing mark of Christ's followers. "By this everyone will know that you are my disciples, if you have love for one another" (John 13:35). Our Lord's teaching, then, places our experience of Christian community at the very heart of the church's life and ministry.

A most baffling aspect of this teaching, however, is how such a *fundamental* and *simple* truth to understand can be so *rare* and *difficult* to experience.

Community Is Easy to Understand

This truth is *fundamental* in that the close personal relationships that characterize Christian koinonia are at one and the same time Life producing for those who are part of our Christian community, *and* Life producing for those beyond who find such relationships so attractive. Koinonia is an "evangelizing fellowship"—Life for ourselves and Life for others. You see, if we are experiencing *real* Christian fellowship, *real* sharing and caring, we are an inviting, attractive group to those beyond ourselves.

So this truth is foundational, basic to Christian Life and Mission: Love for one another benefits those in our church and attracts those outside our church.

Then, too, this truth is fairly *simple* to grasp: It means we seek and foster close personal relationships—relationships characterized by openness and acceptance, warmth and growth. It is sharing at a deeper, more personal level than chitchat or socializing. It is taking time with a small group of people to listen and care and pray about what matters most to us: our dreams and hopes, our failures and joys.

Though this teaching is *foundational* and *straightforward*, amazingly, and tragically, we do not practice it often enough in the church today, as community practitioner M. Scott Peck observes in his book *The Different Drum.* Speaking of his upbringing in a Christian home and about his parents, Peck notes:

> They were good American "rugged individualists," and they very clearly wanted me to be one also. The problem was that I was not free to be me. Secure though it was, my home was not a place where it was safe for me to be anxious, afraid, depressed, or dependent—to be myself. . . .
>
> Had someone asked my parents whether they had friends, they would have replied, "Do we have friends? Good gracious, yes. Why, we get over a thousand Christmas cards every Christmas." On one level that answer would have been quite correct.

They led a most active social life and were widely and deservedly respected—even loved. Yet in the deepest definition of the word, I am not sure they had any friends at all. Friendly acquaintances by the droves, yes, but no truly intimate friends. Nor would they have wanted any. They neither desired nor trusted intimacy. Moreover, as far as I can see, in an age of rugged individualism they were quite typical of their time and culture.

But I was left with a nameless longing. I dreamed that somewhere there would be a girl, a woman, a mate with whom I could be totally honest and open, and have a relationship in which the whole of me would be acceptable. That was romantic enough. But what seemed impossibly romantic was an inchoate longing for a society in which honesty and openness would prevail. I had no reason to believe that such a society existed—or ever had existed or ever could exist—until accidently (or by grace) I began to stumble into varieties of real community.[3]

Peck goes on to describe a few rare instances of stumbling into community. And then he says a very disturbing thing:

On my lecture tours across the country the one constant I have found wherever I go—the Northeast, Southeast, Midwest, Southwest, or West Coast—is the lack—and the thirst for—community. This lack and thirst is particularly heartbreaking in those places where one might expect to find real community: in churches. . . .

In our culture of rugged individualism—in which we generally feel that we dare not be honest about ourselves, even with the person in the pew next to us—we bandy around the word "community." We apply it to almost any collection of individuals—a town, a church, a synagogue, a fraternal organization, an apartment complex, a professional association—regardless of how poorly those individuals communicate with each other. It is a false use of the word.

If we are going to use the word meaningfully we must restrict it to a group of individuals who have learned how to communicate honestly with each other, whose relationships go

deeper than their masks of composure, and who have developed
some significant commitment to "rejoice together, mourn together," and to "delight in each other, make others' conditions
our own." But what, then, does such a rare group look like?
How does it function? What is a true definition of community?[4]

Of course there are a number of dictionary definitions of *community*, which can refer to *place* as well as to *relationships*. For our discussions in this handbook, *community* refers to people who interact interper-
sonally in a locality. Clearly the emphasis is on our sense of community
rather than on the place where we experience it. More specifically, I will
focus on the relational dimension of community and consider *close personal relationships* as the essence of a sense of community.

Peck goes on to identify several qualities of true Christian community, including inclusiveness—all of us are welcome; commitment to one
another, including appreciation of our differences; making decisions by
mutual agreement; and an atmosphere of realism, of growth, and of safe-
ty to be ourselves. He says, for example, that

> community is a safe place precisely because no one is attempting
> to heal or convert you, to fix you, to change you. Instead, the
> members accept you as you are. You are free to be you. And
> being so free, you are free to discard defenses, masks, disguises;
> free to seek your own psychological and spiritual health; free to
> become your whole and holy self.[5]

Perhaps the most startling thing Peck says is that "the most successful community in this nation—probably in the whole world—is Alcohol-
ics Anonymous, the 'Fellowship of AA.'"[6]

But real community need not be limited to people in recovery, as in
AA. In the larger population it need not be found only by "accident," as
Peck described his finds. The church can *design* or *create* it! Intentional
community can be part of our normal, everyday lives, contribute to our
wholeness, even prevent or minimize our crises.

Peck himself has learned that community can be created. In recent
years he has traveled around the country offering community-building
workshops, presenting guidelines for communication and community
that can be simply taught and easily learned. Peck says, "In other words,

if they know what they are doing, virtually any group of people can form themselves into a genuine community."[7]

Distinguished pastor and preacher John Claypool tells of the event that introduced him to genuine community. One day a colleague invited him to join a koinonia group:

> He was in real personal anguish, he said, and he asked the question: "Where does a pastor go for pastoral care? We are so busy helping other people. Where do we turn when our needs become overwhelming?
>
> "At any rate," he continued, "I am calling five of you whom I trust with this request. Would you agree to meet with me in my study once a week for six times? The only contract will be that we will try to be honest and hear each other. Perhaps we can develop enough trust so that we can take off our masks and show each other where we really hurt. And maybe we can become a band of brothers who can bequeath healing and encouragement to each other. I do not know if this will work, but if it does not, I'll go under for sure!"

Claypool reflects on his response:

> I was frankly startled when that conversation was over, because I had only known this man from a distance, and he appeared to be "so together" that I could never have dreamed in a thousand years that he was struggling. . . . So the next morning I went to that man's study and touched for the first time in my life an experience of genuine *koinonia*. I was absolutely astonished by what began to unfold before my eyes. For one thing, I discovered that every one of us around that table was struggling with much the same problems. Miguel Unamuno, the Spanish philosopher, once said that if we ever got honest enough to go out in the streets and uncover our common grief, we would discover that we are all grieving for the selfsame things.

Claypool concludes:

> We were all so much more alike than I had realized. Then, too, I

was amazed to see that in that context honesty evoked compas-
sion. Whenever a person was authentic enough to take off his
mask and let his true condition be seen, instead of being con-
demned or exploited, I found all kinds of insight and concern
flowed to him as response.[8]

Near the beginning of my campus ministry in the mid-1960s, I felt
the need to connect with other helping professionals. I suspected several
colleagues, like myself, were giving a great deal of themselves to others
without having enough care or support to sustain their work. So I phoned
another campus minister, a nurse, and a parish pastor. I explained that I
was in dire need of people to listen to my concerns, to help me gain perspective, and to pray for me. My hunch was correct: Each of them had
similar needs with no prospect of help.

I took the initiative and scheduled our first support group meeting.
For the two years I served in this locale, we found the care and support
and prayer we all needed from meeting weekly with one another.

In each of the four places I've served since that time, I have taken a
similar initiative for similar reasons with similar results. Some groups
were mostly colleagues; other groups included parishioners and were
part of my church's small-group ministry. My wife, also a parish pastor,
participated in some of these groups and not in others. For me, I know I
could not have succeeded in my personal or professional life without
participating in a sharing or support group. It's just that critical to my
survival and well-being.

Community Is Hard to Experience

Why is genuine Christian community so *rare*? Why are there so few
places where the church is a contagious, alive, and attractive evangelizing fellowship? Why is this inviting quality of life where Christians love
one another such a *difficult* part of our faith to experience? In short, why
does so little genuine community exist among us?

Our *problem* of community, which noted sociologist Robert Nisbet
calls the single most impressive fact in twentieth-century Western society, is relatively modern. For most of our human history, group life was a
given. But we have less and less reason to be together and fewer and

fewer ways of knowing each other, while our need for intimate, interpersonal relationships remains constant.

Community scholars concur in describing contemporary society as alienated, rootless, lonely, and lacking a sense of belonging. While belonging, not escape, is the current imperative moral value, people have a war within themselves between aloneness and community. On the one hand, people today feel they do not need each other. People who do know one another are rarely neighbors. On the other hand, while people seek community, they are scared of it and are fearful of getting too close to others. This current relational malaise is heightened because most of us will never get back to the extended family, the parish, and the village of earlier life. For most people, finding a place where it is safe to be known is simply not attainable.

If community scholars concur that the paramount contemporary problem of Western society concerns regaining our lost sense of community, they are not in agreement when it comes to the cause of our predicament. For example, pastoral theologian Charles Gerkin believes too many churches are clergy-oriented and thus restricted in their ability to develop relational community among the congregation as a whole and reach out to the world.[9] Psychologist Evelyn Eaton Whitehead and pastoral theologian James Whitehead suggest that our contemporary crisis in community stems from ambiguity or confusion in the distinction between issues such as diversity and unity, pluralism and individualism, and the definition of community as a psychological quality or a social structure.[10] Psychologist Seymour Sarason believes that where community has failed, that failure usually has the following four internal sources: a lack of continuing felt need for community, a forgetting to continue the inner community relationships, a closure to outsiders, or an attitude of "ought to" rather than "want to."[11]

While clergy style and ambiguity in our thinking about community are surely important concerns, the internal, relational causes suggested by Sarason seem more to the point.

And the church can provide solutions to these internal, relational problems. Community scholar Paul Hanson finds community as the unifying theme of the Hebrew Bible and of the New Testament, where God calls people into a community of faith as a covenant-people.[12]

Community Is Possible through the Church

Because the church contains a greater cross section of people than any other institution,[13] the church has an unparalleled opportunity and responsibility to contribute to the solution of our pressing societal problem of the relationship gap. More specifically, the church can be an alternative community that models God's intended relationship with humanity in the world.[14]

As children of God we may struggle with the "relationship problem," but we confess that "we need one another."

Hanson puts it this way:

> It would be inaccurate to characterize the members of a true community of faith as solitary heroes of righteousness in the world. In fact, the faithful in the Bible are not portrayed as invincible individuals capable of single-handedly vanquishing the foe. Moses, Jeremiah, and Jesus are portrayed as humans with genuine needs for comfort, encouragement, and support. In creating community, God has graciously provided for a deep human need.[15]

Pastoral psychologist Robert Leslie brings broader focus to the value of the small groups in a congregation when he says: "In a culture in which intimate personal relationships are increasingly harder to find, the church can serve a distinctive role by providing a structure for small sharing groups."[16] Like Bonhoeffer,[17] Leslie reminds us that care for one another in the Christian community must always be seen against the backdrop of our higher loyalty to the word of God in Christ.

Hanson affirms:

> The biblical notion of being in the world begins with supportive community, where the faithful can gather to celebrate all that is good and worthy in life as a gift of divine grace, and can commemorate the central events of their common spiritual history together, like the event of deliverance from slavery in the Jewish passover, or the events of rebirth and atonement in Christian baptism and the eucharist.[18]

Such affirmation provides an external frame of reference and makes our church groups different from secular groups. Without such an external standard of judgment, even our intimate, supportive groups may be effectively therapeutic for our own members but oblivious to any external standard.[19] Leslie captures well the contribution made by personal sharing groups in the church, meeting in Christ's name, when he remarks:

> That God might stand in judgment on the process, that God might have a claim on [people] prior to the claim of the group, that the horizontal dimensions of life are meaningful only in terms of a transcendent God who stands outside of the life of [humankind]—all this can be lost sight of in a group that stresses only the meeting of its own personal needs. Yet in the very act of keeping God in the picture, of making [God] the central loyalty, a new awareness of the significance of relationships emerges. Indeed the gospel can be read largely as a matter of relationships.[20]

Concludes Leslie:

> God is not found in objective law, in sterile formulas, in impersonal rules. God is found in participation, in involvement, in celebration. God is found in relationships, in encounters, in the joys and sorrows of human experience, in the give and take of dialogue. In the miracle of relatedness we discover that we are no longer strangers, but members together in a household, bound together in our common loyalty to God.[21]

The Paradox of Community

Peck suggests that while we want intimacy, we run from it. Perplexing, isn't it? We want to be honest and open, but we are not willing to risk being ourselves in a group of sisters and brothers.

Let's say that Greg is upset over his teenager's recent experimentation with smoking pot. He wants help to sort out his feelings but is reluctant to say so. Brandy notices Greg's ambivalence when he tells the group he had a "routine week." But when Brandy inquires, "You sure you feel okay today, Greg? You seem a little down to me," Greg answers, "No, everything is going fine, really!" Unable to be honest, Greg fools only himself and agonizes in his own silent world.

If and when we are honest with ourselves, we know we need other people. While the rugged individualism of our time surely runs counter to this reality, there are additional issues that we often overlook.

The Issue of Confidentiality

Lack of trust—or the issue of confidentiality—is one factor that helps us explain this push-pull paradox. Fear of exposure can prevent people, particularly those who live in small town and rural areas, from joining koinonia groups in the first place. Grapevine communication is so pervasive in many small communities and rural areas that people guard themselves against revealing personal information with virtually anyone. Why should we in the church expect to be any different from the community-at-large in risking self-disclosure?

Overcoming such a deeply ingrained and often well-founded fear is not an easy accomplishment for planners of community. Assurance of confidentiality is needed before many will even consider joining a small group, and it is a ground rule a group should adopt and follow right from the start. Even so, it may take a long time and considerable evidence that trust is warranted for many church members to risk self-disclosure.

The Issue of Truth

A second factor influencing this push-pull dynamic of intimacy is the difficulty we human beings have in *facing the truth* about ourselves. How often we wear masks and try to cover our tracks. How easily we deceive ourselves and others and try to justify inappropriate behavior. When we are afraid to face our true selves and when we deceive others, we tend to flee relationships—with God, with ourselves, and also with others.

This urge to go it alone is not the only result of our deceptions; they can also prevent us from developing trust even if confidentiality is assured and practiced. If we conceal rather than risk disclosing our true selves, and if we deceive rather than trust others, we prevent the two necessary conditions for experiencing intimacy in our relationships: risk and trust.

What gives us the freedom to face the truth about ourselves? The Christian gospel affirms that it is okay not to be okay. Jesus came preaching a message of repentance and forgiveness of sin. Repent and believe in the gospel, Jesus taught. God's unconditional acceptance of us is what can give us the freedom to face the truth about ourselves—to be our true selves, warts and all. Rather than flee from others, then, we become free to reveal our shortcomings, to acknowledge our need for others' acceptance and support and care, and to change our ways. Rather than deceiving others, we can risk opening ourselves so that trust and intimacy can develop in our interpersonal relationships.

The following story about Father Elias Chacour of Galilee illustrates the impact of forgiveness. It also demonstrates the power that facing the truth accompanied by forgiveness has in restoring or recreating Christian community—*love for one another*, which Jesus says will be the means by which the world will come to know we are Jesus' disciples.

The story is told by Jim Forest and based on an interview with Father Chacour:

> Not only among Palestinians, but also among many Jews, he has become one of the most respected people of northern Israel. Now, through his autobiography, *Blood Brothers*, he is becoming well known in many countries.
>
> Elias lives in Ibillin, an ancient hilltop village near Haifa surrounded by olive trees, some of them older than Christianity. Today his congregation is thriving. They have built a regional high school, opened a community centre, and established a large library. In the library is a beautiful sign in Arabic with this text:
>
> *God is the creator of all human beings, with their difference, their colours, their races, their religions. Be attentive: Every time you draw nearer to your neighbour, you draw nearer to God. Be attentive: Every time you go further from your neighbour, you go further from God.*

When Elias was first sent to that town many years ago, there was no community centre or library and neighbours were far apart. The church was falling down and the small congregation that worshipped inside was in no better condition than the building. The divisions that ran through the parish could be seen in the way that people arranged themselves in the church on Sunday: four distinct groups each keeping a distance from the others, and everyone with grim faces. The fundamental division in the church was between four brothers; even the death of their mother had not provided the occasion for the brothers to be in the same room together.

On Palm Sunday of his first year as pastor of Ibillin, Elias looked from the front of the church at the stony faces before him. One of the brothers, a policeman, sat in the front row with his wife and children. Hymns were sung, but without any spirit. There were readings from the Bible, and then a sermon. "The congregation endured me indifferently," Elias recalls, "fulfilling their holiday obligation to warm the benches." But before the service ended, he did something no one, not even he himself, had anticipated. He walked to the back of the church and padlocked the door.

Returning to the front of the church, he told his parishioners, "Sitting in this building does not make you a Christian. You are a people divided. You argue and hate each other. You gossip and spread lies. Your religion is a lie. If you can't love your brother whom you can see, how can you say that you love God who is invisible? You have allowed the Body of Christ to be disgraced. I have tried for months to unite you. I have failed. I am only a man. But there is someone else who can bring you together in true unity. His name is Jesus. He has the power to forgive you. So now I will be quiet and allow him to give you that power. If you will not forgive, then we stay locked in here. If you want, you can kill each other, and I'll provide your funeral gratis."

Ten minutes passed, but for Elias they seemed like hours. At last the policeman stood up, faced the congregation, bowed his head, and said, "I am sorry. I am the worst of all. I have hated my own brothers. I have hated them so much that I wanted to kill them. More than any of you, I need forgiveness."

He turned to Elias. "Father, can you forgive me?" "Come here," Elias replied. They embraced each other with the kiss of peace. "Now go and greet your brothers."

The four brothers rushed together, meeting halfway down the aisle, and in tears forgave each other. "In an instant," Elias recalls, "the church was a chaos of embracing and repentance."

Elias had to shout to make his next words audible. "Dear friends, we are not going to wait until next week to celebrate the Resurrection. Let us begin it now. We were dead to each other. Now we are alive again." He began to sing, "Christ is risen from the dead. By his death he has trampled death and given life to those in the tombs." The congregation joined in the hymn. Unchaining the door, Elias led them into the streets.

"For the rest of the day and into the evening, I joined groups of believers as they went from house to house. At every door, someone had to ask forgiveness for a certain wrong. Never was forgiveness withheld."[22]

The Issue of Church Size

Besides confidentiality and facing the truth, *church size* can also be an obstacle that keeps us from realizing our desire to experience authentic Christian community. Our culture overly enamors a bigger-is-better mentality.

When a church is small, say with fewer than thirty members, it may be able to function as one large relational circle. But when a church gets much bigger than that, there isn't "room" for everyone to experience the openness, acceptance, warmth, and personal growth possible in the smaller community. This means that as a church increases in size, leaders must be *intentional* in planning and taking necessary steps to develop multiple groups to maintain a sense of Christian community.[23]

Numbers do matter: We cannot develop sufficiently close personal relationships in large groups. Relational development literature, in fact, tells us that it is difficult to experience intimacy in our interpersonal relationships in groups of more than six to ten people. Consequently, unless we plan and develop new or additional opportunities for group life, we severely curb both our Christian koinonia and our outreach to others.

The Issue of Time Management

Our crowded schedules may also limit creation of Christian community in our congregations. Unless we drop some current commitment, project, or amusement, many of us simply cannot add another meeting to our schedules.

Over the years I have worked to rearrange my schedule so as to maintain balance and sanity. When I was a college teacher, I did a great deal of consulting in churches outside my regular work. It just got to be too much after a while. So when I came to my present pastoral position, I negotiated with my church to allow me a half day a week for the teaching I wanted to do at a nearby theological seminary. This meant that I could include part of my "outside work" in my regular work schedule. It made a great deal of difference in my overall well-being. While I do quite well in taking time for myself—fishing, reading, support group, and so forth—after several years in my current situation I found my home and family time suffering. So I declined a second term on one of the community service boards I've served on and said no to service on a new denominational committee. I also cut back my work week from fifty-four to forty-five hours over a three-year period. With these adjustments and vigilant monitoring, my life feels back in balance once again.

Rearranging time commitments is a challenge that needs to be confronted if community is to become a priority. Again, desiring community is only half the equation—the need or "pull" to intimacy. The "push" away from intimacy can be as simple as an overscheduled calendar.

Summary

What is the possibility of community in the church?

My studies and experience confirm that the *majority* of people in churches of all sizes desires *more* close personal relationships. As one person said, "Life is too difficult to face alone. I have plenty of friends but not enough people around whom I can drop my guard and really 'tell it like it is.'"

I've also discovered that a *majority* of people in our churches would like to participate in a sharing or support group. In fact, there may be dawning in our society a renewed sense of the importance of experiencing the close personal relationships that the small caring group can provide. While most community sociologists and psychologists report that people today have a "pursuit of loneliness," the majority of church members in my research project reported a desire for more close personal relationships. And in view of those who suggest that only *some* church members have a special interest in sharing with others at a personal level, I found that the majority of church members desires to participate in a personal sharing group.[24]

In view of the role of koinonia—sharing Life together—in enabling church members to love one another, demonstrating that they are Christ's disciples, this is strikingly good news!

In sum, the *importance* of small group life *is* seen in the church. And the *desire* for more small groups is present. But we must address complicating causes of ambivalence, such as concern for confidentiality, facing the truth, church size, and time management if we are to be effective in our efforts to create Christian community.

Beyond the problem and the paradoxes of forming community, there is promise that a sense of community can develop in your church through your small-group ministry. Just how this promise can become a reality in your church is the subject of chapter 2, which completes "The Context" (section 1) for understanding, experiencing, and creating community through small groups.

My study and experience of building Christian community point to careful *planning* (section 2) and to leadership *training* (section 3) as the primary components of an effective small-group ministry. With proper attention to these two elements, a church can overcome these obstacles and experience the intimacy that enables it to be the lively, contagious community Christ desires it to be.

I think you can realistically expect to see one-third to one-half of your congregation actively participate in your small-group ministry after one year, and two-thirds or more within two or three years. In short, *expansion* of your church's small-group ministry can be the medium to create Christian community in your congregation.

The possibility of community in the church looks very good, indeed. This is a truly exciting prospect!

CHAPTER 2

Creating Christian Community through Small Groups

Christian community can make your church come alive!

A genuine sense of community is contagious. For when we in the body of Christ share ourselves with one another in small groups, the Spirit works through us to create an inviting, attractive quality of life. Little wonder, when we remember *the* distinguishing mark of Christ's followers: "By this everyone will know that you are my disciples, if you have love for one another" (John 13:35).

It would seem, then, that the way we Christians treat one another, the quality of our Life together, is a critically important element in the church.

Consider what happened when a medium-sized northwestern Presbyterian church expanded its small-group ministry. Its efforts have produced a lively, ministering congregation. One member, Kyle, tells his story of what he found in one of that church's small groups:

> After my hospitalization for mental illness brought on by the stress of my divorce and bankruptcy, I decided to join one of my church's sharing and support groups. Over time, the acceptance I experienced from the other members of my sharing and support group helped me restore the self-confidence which I had lost. I found a freedom to share my story without fear of judgment or breach of confidentiality, and I received the support I hoped for from the other members of my small group. Before joining the group I felt alone and abandoned, but through the group's warmth I experienced a sense of belonging and human connection again. As my group prayed for me and the needs in my life, I began to notice improvements in my life which amazed me. And it really astonished

people who knew me before, even some in the group itself, when I discovered gifts for ministry and actually became a church officer as a result.

In short, through his sharing and support group, Kyle found healing, care, value, and opportunity to serve others.

Another small group in the church met weekly to share, listen, care, give insight, and pray for one another. From this love-in-action—this genuine Christian community—members received support at the deepest levels of their lives. But eventually the group's influence reached beyond the group. When one member casually mentioned to a mother at a preschool cooperative how much she valued the group, the mother felt drawn to what she heard about the group's quality of life. She asked for more information about this Life and together with her family joined this church and one of its small groups.

A nurse in the same group reports a similar experience:

While listening to a patient recount the depression and loneliness of her life, I just naturally commented that I find acceptance, support, and belonging from the members of my small group. My patient was just amazed, really impressed, and asked for more information about the quality of caring and meaning in life I find in my group.

Another of this church's small groups, a peace-making mission group, led a worship service in which they told about their study of peace and justice and their vision for peace making. They even invited the congregation to join them in their peace-making work. Members of the congregation were not the only ones to benefit from what they heard; several visitors were moved by this service and felt attracted to the church's life and ministry.

These examples illustrate the impact small groups can have in your church's life. Many new members have joined this church since it expanded its small-group ministry. When asked why, most of these new members said that they were drawn by the opportunity to join a small group. These examples also demonstrate how your congregation can become a "group of small groups,"[1] and how your worship life can become a natural extension or expression of your church's small-group ministry. After all, this is what Christian community, *koinonia*, is all about—sharing Life together in the body of Christ, and reaching out to those beyond our churches.[2]

But how can this inviting quality of life express itself in your church? How can your congregation function as an accepting, supportive, and caring fellowship? How can a sense of Christian community develop in your church?

The Role of Small Groups in Creating Christian Community

Church consultant Lyle Schaller suggests that many small congregations can be thought of as a large small group; healthy medium and large congregations have many small face-to-face groups (i.e., classes, circles, clubs, fellowships, associations, choirs, cliques, committees, boards, commissions, task forces, and work areas).[3] Schaller makes the following insightful observation:

> In the small congregation of sixty confirmed members, the principal primary face-to-face group may include three-quarters of the confirmed members plus several children. In the 30-member congregation this face-to-face caring fellowship may include five-sixths of the members plus some nonmembers, while in the congregation of 200 confirmed members this central fellowship circle is unlikely to include as many as one-half of the members.
>
> In simple terms this means that in the smaller congregations the primary face-to-face group is likely to include a far larger proportion of the members than in the middle-sized and large churches. It also means that in the smaller churches the congregations, "as a congregation," can function as a caring, supportive and redemptive fellowship. In the large church this goal can be accomplished only through group life, and not by the congregation attempting to act as one large fellowship.[4]

My study and experience tell me that even small congregations with a caring circle of twenty to thirty members push the limits of effective community. In such "large small groups" most people are hesitant to engage in the intimate personal sharing that community building requires. Such sharing usually takes place only in groups of six to twelve. So it is through our small groups, then, that primary, face-to-face, supportive and caring relationships best occur. In fact, a genuine sense of community can develop in most of our congregations only through our small-group ministries.

Pastoral psychologist Robert Leslie supports this view and maintains that the small group can provide the medium for the kind of personal sharing and spiritual renewal that so many of us yearn for in an otherwise fractured world.[5] Similarly, church consultant Roy Oswald claims that, especially in our larger congregations, parishioners are best able to meet their needs and experience renewal through personal support groups.[6] Pastoral psychologist Howard Clinebell also affirms that such groups are the most effective means for involving the maximum number of people: "In the small, sharing group lies the power which enables persons to love more fully and live more creatively. This power is the people dynamic—'the power we have to recreate each other and ourselves through caring and sharing.'"[7]

A small-group ministry can be the primary means by which your congregation expresses its life and mission. No matter what activities are prominent in a group (sharing, study, prayer, celebration, mission, and so forth), it is the quality of Christian "life together"—Christian community—that brings Life for ourselves and draws people outside our church to ask: "What is going on here? This life is attractive and I'd like to experience it too!" It is at this point that verbalization of the gospel makes sense—as an explanation for the quality of life among us as Christians, the *koinonia*, Christian community.

Indeed, we can have confidence in the role small groups play in creating a sense of Christian community in our congregations. The examples earlier in this chapter from a church that makes small groups the primary means of expressing its life and mission illustrate the covenantal notion of binding together to find Life so that we may share Life with those beyond the church.[8]

Richard Halverson, veteran pastor and long-time U.S. Senate chaplain, poignantly sums up the role of small groups in creating a sense of Christian community in our congregations:

In the apostolic church, the relationship between believers and God and between [other] believers was paramount. The forgiving and

accepting spirit that emanated from the unique community pen-
etrated a jaded, bored, loveless, weary culture and awakened the
spiritual hunger of both Jew and pagan. It was said of them, "Lo,
how they love one another!" Sin-sick fed up [people] tried to
understand the strange and inviting quality of life that marked the
disciples.[9]

Some Significant Observations on Small Groups in the Church

The following observations, gleaned from Robert Leslie's expertise on
sharing groups and from my own study and experience of relational
small groups, show what characteristics of a small group create and
promote a sense of community.

How an Effective Small Group Functions

As for group *functioning,* Leslie makes these observations and suggests
these guidelines:[10]

- Sharing groups are relatively small, ranging from eight to eighteen members.

- Group cohesion usually takes a minimum of fifteen to twenty hours to develop.

- A fairly unstructured, agendaless style best fosters member participation and an increase in self-awareness.

- A content-orientation best develops naturally rather than being
formally introduced.

- Study and personal sharing can go hand-in-hand. In fact, the most
natural way for sharing to emerge in small groups is through study;
most people are comfortable coming together as a study group.

The key to most effective study groups is in introducing the note of personal sharing.

* Communication is more the goal than socializing; interaction is on a meaningful level and members freely, without defensiveness, listen and talk on a personal level.

* When creating new sharing groups, some church members may not show an initial interest in participating and taking such a personal risk. The best groups are nurtured rather than organized into being. Attempts to organize whole parishes into small sharing groups that overlook this important factor may doom the program to failure before it begins. Because sharing groups require an interest in relating at a personal level, some screening may need to be done to bring together those who are eager to participate without precipitating resistance from those who are not ready to be open because of anxiety.[11]

* Members must accept responsibility for group life, involving a "disciplined spontaneity" in which each member takes into account other people's needs and recognizes that becoming a genuine person implies being a person-in-community.

* Focus should be on the present without ignoring the past; the past clarifies the present.

* Give preference to personal sharing over diagnostic probing; self-disclosure of feelings is always appropriate, but the exploration of others' motives is not.

* Give freedom for spontaneous expressions of feeling if people claim their feelings as their own and offer them in a mood of openness and corroboration. Observations are welcome; personal attacks are not.

* Everyone participates, including the leader whom the group experiences as a human being struggling with problems just as everyone else.

- Growth and change occur not by compulsion but by a combination of understanding acceptance and gentle challenge.

- Action beyond the group is expected and shared; the developing openness, flexibility, responsibility, and growth in group members becomes a leavening influence outside the group, and the group provides a support base for sharing the experiences, frustrations, and satisfactions of the journey outward.[12]

I add my own observations about group functioning to those of Robert Leslie:

1. A very simple agenda can lead group members to the most important experience of their lives.

- The simple question, "What's been happening in your life this past week?" can lead group members to talk about what matters most to them.

- Usually, after a comfortable, supportive, and unhurried atmosphere develops in a small group, very little leadership is needed.

- Emergent, conversational prayer can be a natural, powerful activity following the sharing experience.

2. Certain attitudes or behaviors are particularly helpful for developing a supportive group climate.

- Showing interest in one another's concerns allows a trust and vitality to emerge in a group's life. Such genuine, active interest helps us know we are taken seriously and leads to support for working through our concerns.

- When it becomes okay to say what we want, in the way we want, when we experience a nonjudgmental attitude from other group members, we sense a tremendous "liberation"—freedom to be ourselves.

- Our most satisfying supportive relationships seem to develop
  when we experience openness, acceptance, warmth, and personal
  growth.[13]

- A supportive group atmosphere in which we can most be ourselves
  usually develops from group activity that is sharing oriented in-,
  formal, feeling oriented, and neither too structured nor too rigidly
  led.

- We can diminish feelings of personal threat or defensiveness in our
  interpersonal relations when we are descriptive rather than evalu-
  ative, caring rather than controlling, spontaneous rather than strategic, empathic rather than neutral, equal rather than superior, and
  open to change rather than close-minded.[14]

3. Groups generally profit from initiating, developing, and terminat-
    ing their own agreements about group life.

- Sharing, study, prayer, and mission are typical group activities.
  These elements might vary among groups and over the course of a
  group's life. It is especially important that all members have enthu-
  siasm for and commitment to the group's activities; in fact, if in -
  terests are too divergent, it is probably better to divide into several
  groups with different activities.

- Groups can form in a number of ways: (1) around one person's
  vision, (2) around the common interests of several people, or (3)
  around the geographic assignment of members to groups. With this
  third method of group formation, the emergence of a common
  vision and commitment to group life may be difficult to establish,
  requiring exceedingly skillful group leadership. Today people who
  know one another well are rarely neighbors. Because a sense of
  community does not seem to develop along geographic lines, it is
  best to *not* form groups according to zones.[15]   Relationships —
  over time and variety of interests rather than locale per se are
  probably the key factors to consider in forming groups.

- When a group grows to be more than ten to twelve members, we need to be aware that intimacy and closeness will necessarily be lost unless we take steps to develop two smaller groups.

4.   When creating or expanding a small-group program, clear biblical and theological foci and careful planning are needed.

•   A centering on the Word is essential for the support and care of close relations among Christians to begin and grow. Such center ing on Jesus Christ reminds us of our identity, our power, and our mission.

   Note that Jesus asked us to celebrate the Lord's Supper in re- membrance of him, perhaps because he knew our tendency to for- get. How fickle our memories can be! Such remembering helps anchor us to our tradition and keeps us from becoming so self- centered and present-oriented that we forget whose we are, from where our power comes, and what our mission is.[16] Such anchor ing also helps us remember to be inclusive and welcoming to all rather than turned in on ourselves, oblivious to others' need for a sense of community, and closed to newcomers.[17]

•   The process of developing and adopting a purpose, goals, and a strategy is vitally important. All church leaders need to participate in this formulation process—to adopt and present to the congrega- tion a common mission and understanding of the plan.[18]

•   Besides providing training and support for potential small-group leaders, a church needs to develop plans for continual assessment and presentation of the program.

How an Effective Small Group Is Led

As for *leading* sharing groups, Leslie suggests that the leader:[19]

•   Establish the tone and climate for group life using a catalyst rather than authoritarian style.

•   Strive to create a growth-producing climate rather than become the expert by being a group facilitator[20] rather than a therapist.[21]

- Model group participation as well as provide focus and direction for group interaction.

- Focus more on feeling than rationality even though much cognitive learning occurs.

- Serve as a resource person when necessary.

Leslie also says a group leader has the primary responsibility to see that the group experiences:

- sufficient structure
- feedback
- personal involvement
- empathy, warmth, and genuineness
- confidence in groups
- shared leadership
- nudging toward change
- linkage between the group experience and Christian faith.

Again, I add my own findings about leadership to Leslie's. I summarize my observations in one sentence: **The person designated as group leader is typically the key to an effective small group, especially early in a group's life.**

- The leader is a member of the group who helps the group go where it wants to go to the extent that it needs such help.

- Early in a group's life, the leader can be especially helpful in assisting the group in establishing its purpose and agreements about group life, in building a supportive group climate, and in making suggestions for member participation.

- In ongoing group life, group leadership usually functions to facilitate group interaction so that group purposes are accomplished. Such leadership may be provided by one person or may be shared by several members.

- Adequate training must be provided for potential small-group leaders. A six- to ten-week training course should be sufficient, depending on the candidate's abilities and experience. A leaders' support group can be an important means of continuing training, mutual support, and coordination of overall strategy once inauguration or expansion of a small-group program is underway.

Summary

Small groups play a central role in creating community in the church. To illustrate how Christian community can make our churches come alive through small groups, this chapter began with real-life examples from a church's small-group ministry.

The significant observations provided guidelines and insights to help us see just how small groups produce a sense of Christian community.

Section 1, "The Context," is now complete. We have perspective for understanding and experiencing Christian community and realize the central role small groups play in creating it.

Next, then, let's move to the heart of this handbook: section 2, "The Planning," and section 3, "The Training."

The Planning

CHAPTER 3

Creating a Plan

Like two wings on an airplane, planning and training are essential components of an effective small-group ministry. Well-planned small-group programs that are not accompanied by proper training for potential small-group leaders are likely to fail because so many of our lay leaders do not know how to lead an effective small group. Conversely, programs with well-trained group leaders but without proper planning are not likely to be effective because the process of implementing new small groups is complex, requiring careful organization. Theologically speaking, the gifts of administration and equipping are as essential for an effective small-group ministry as for other ministries in the church.

You will find three components of well-planned small-group ministries in this three-chapter section. In this chapter we will cover the critical elements of a steering committee, a purpose, goals, and a strategy for your small-group program.

Forming a Steering Committee

The first task in creating an effective small-group ministry is to form a steering committee. (This is especially important in the large and medium-sized church. Small churches where leaders work as a committee-of-the-whole may find it best for current leaders to assume the steering committee functions. Likewise, small churches with few committees and few available committee members may satisfactorily assign small-group oversight to an existing committee.) Right at the beginning, you'll need to clearly determine a steering committee's task, duration, and accountability.

Committee Task

As for *task*: Your steering committee will normally assume responsibility
for developing and facilitating a process to *expand* your church's small-
group ministry. You should note that I use the term *expand* rather than
begin. This word choice is important because small groups already exist
in most churches, e.g., study groups, prayer groups. Considering this, it
is presumptuous, even arrogant, for a steering committee to oversee a
church's *new* small-group ministry. It is more accurate to think in terms
of enlarging the church's small-group ministry.

Committee Duration

As for the committee's *duration*: Consider your committee a standing
committee if you conceive of your small-group program as ongoing and
central to your congregation's life and mission.

Discussing the committee's duration requires more specific delinea-
tion of its "developing and facilitating" task. After your initial planning
(establishing purpose, goals, and strategy) is complete, the committee's
task turns to recruiting potential small-group leaders; then to planning
and conducting a group leaders' training course; then to planning and
implementing the small-group program's presentation to the congregation. After you add new groups to your existing ones, you will need to
provide ongoing program coordination and leader support. Indeed, your
steering committee's functions are numerous and continuous throughout
the life of your church's small-group ministry.

Committee Accountability

As for steering committee *accountability*: Where your committee fits
into your church's overall mission and organizational structure is probably less important than the fact that it *has* a body that mandates, over-
sees, and supports its work. Typical bodies are the church's membership, fellowship, or education committees. Don't be surprised if the
parent body has only a general idea of the purpose of a small-group
ministry or a steering committee.

Steps for Setting Up a Steering Committee

The initiating or parent body should find two or three qualified laypeople, a staff person, and, if necessary, a small-group ministry resource person or consultant to begin the planning process. Then let this ad hoc group of interested people draft (1) a statement of small-group ministry purpose, goals, and strategy and (2) a steering committee job description. Submit these drafts to the initiating body for review and approval and then to the church's primary decision-making body for adoption. Now it's time to appoint the small-group ministry steering committee, which will begin its work of expanding your congregation's small-group program. In all probability, your ad hoc group appointed to draft the original expansion proposals will continue as your ongoing steering committee.

Do not underestimate the importance of these steps! Unless your church leaders understand and wholeheartedly affirm the role small groups will play in your congregation, and unless they process the draft statements in such a way that they "own" them, you set yourself up for possible failure. If your small-group program is to be central to your church's life and ministry, your church leaders must decide that its small-group ministry purpose, goals, and strategy are sound and worth supporting.

Committee Membership and Size

An interest and confidence in small groups are vital qualities for your initial ad hoc group and your ongoing steering committee members. Prospective members should have a real desire to see small groups become central to your church's ministry. Likewise, they should believe in the value small groups can bring to your congregation's life and mission.

Other essential qualities for prospective committee members include creativity and organization. You need idea-people to conceptualize and design your ministry. Finally, you need good organizers to coordinate and facilitate your program.

Experience and training in group life are desirable though not essential for planning team members. If prospective lay and clergy members do not have fairly extensive experience and training in developing a small-group ministry, I think you will find that this handbook provides all the resources you require to develop such a ministry.

For ad hoc and steering committee size, I recommend a rather small number of committed, qualified people who are willing to take initiative for the ministry. Two or three laypeople and one staff person are usually enough to form an effective steering committee. Again, your ad hoc group appointed to draft the original expansion proposals may well continue as your ongoing steering committee.

Creating a Purpose

When your ad hoc group creates a general statement of the overall reason for the small-group ministry's existence, think in terms of what the program should accomplish and how it can do so. What are the program's general ends and means?

I find this process works well to generate ideas for the ministry purpose: Have each ad hoc group member work alone to draft a purpose statement; then members can compare statements. The group can write a consensus statement as it discusses and sifts common and unique elements of these statements.

One church adopted this small-group ministry purpose statement: "To provide opportunities for nurture and growth of all members, so that as a sense of community is developed and expressed, we may live out Christ in our lives."

Another church stated its purpose this way: "To be a vehicle by which the whole congregation is welcomed and actively involved in the growth of ourselves and our faith, the nurture of our community, and the expansion of the work of Christ."

Note the presence of both the *means* and the *ends* of these programs. The first: By providing opportunities for nurture and growth of all members where a sense of community is developed and expressed (the means), Christ is lived out in members' lives (the end). The second: By being a vehicle by which the whole congregation can feel welcome and involved (the means), the small-group ministry can result in member growth, nurture of community, and expansion of Christ's work (the end).

Creating Goals

Goal statements specify how you will accomplish your adopted purpose.
Goal statements, like purpose statements, contain both a means (an
activity) and an end (what an activity can accomplish). Again, have each
person work alone to write goal statements for the small-group ministry.
Then compare notes and examine the unique and common elements of
each person's contribution. If possible, examine goal statements from
other churches. Then develop a consensus statement of reachable goals
to recommend to the appropriate body.

Typical small-group activities (the means) include study, sharing,
prayer, and mission. Other possibilities include personal growth and
celebration. Here are specific, attainable goals that accompany the first
small-group ministry purpose statement presented earlier—"To provide
opportunities for nurture and growth of all members, so that as a sense of
community is developed and expressed, we may live out Christ in our
lives."

1. To provide opportunities for members to discover and learn to
   express their gifts.
2. To provide opportunities for members to share the joys and
   frustrations of daily life in an atmosphere of mutual support and
   care.
3. To provide opportunities for study to increase knowledge of
   Christian life and service.
4. To provide opportunities to experience the power of God in our
   lives by praying for one another.
5. To experience nurture and support in order to express our faith
   in Christ in mission to those beyond the church.

Here are goals developed for the second purpose statement presented earlier—"To be a vehicle by which the whole congregation is
welcomed and actively involved in the growth of ourselves and our faith,
the nurture of our community, and the expansion of the work of Christ."

1. Study—to learn more about Christian faith, life, and service.
2. Self-understanding—to discover greater insights and understand
   ing of ourselves (e.g., feelings, potentials, and gifts).

3. Support—to increase our experience of close personal relationships in which we share the joys and frustrations of daily life.
4. Mission—to express our faith in service to those beyond our
   congregation.
5. Experience of God—to enable us to gain a greater understanding
   and experience of God.

Designing a Strategy

Having drafted purpose and goal statements, you're ready to design a
strategy that describes in detail the tasks to be done to achieve your
goals. Each strategy item should describe a specific action to perform.
Each item should be specific, reachable, and measurable, including dates
for completing tasks.

Here is the actual strategy one ad hoc group designed to produce its
program:

- Select and recruit potential small-group leaders during September
  and October.
- Plan and adopt a training course for potential leaders by early
  October.
- Offer a course in leading small groups for potential small-group
  leaders during late October to mid-December.
- Create and implement plans to interpret the small-group ministry
  to the congregation during December and January.
- Devise and implement a plan to inaugurate new small groups by
  the end of January.
- Plan and provide support for leaders as needed.
- Create a plan for phase 2 (September-December) by May.

The first strategy item is the topic of our next chapter, "Recruiting
Potential Small-Group Leaders." Chapter 5 discusses the second item,
"Planning a Leadership Training Course." The third strategy item is
presented in section 3, chapter 6, "Training Potential Small-Group Leaders." And section 4 covers the remaining strategy items in terms of expansion of a small-group ministry.

CHAPTER 4

Recruiting Potential Small-Group Leaders

Don't underestimate the importance of this phase of your small-group ministry development. How will you call forth people to participate in a training course for your potential small-group leaders? The notions of "call forth," "participate," and "potential" are important here, so let's examine each.

If your small-group ministry is central to your congregation's life and mission, your group leaders have very important roles to play. Effective group leadership requires particular abilities and developed skills. In a word, your ministry thrives on the gift of leadership. This means you need to take much care in recruiting your potential leaders. In fact, selection of potential small-group leaders should receive the same kind of attention as does the selection of church officers.

As you approach prospective leaders, you may discover that some do not think they have enough group leadership training or experience to accept the challenge with confidence. So your first step in recruiting potential small-group leaders is to assure them that you will provide sufficient training for one who is "called forth" to lead effectively—with confidence. Invite potential small-group leaders to participate in your leadership training course. This gives them opportunity and time to discern whether leading a small group is their calling. Granted, this a unique type of calling forth—asking people to participate in training before determining if they'll lead a group—but I find that it does fit many church situations. In chapter 6 it will become apparent that the decision to lead or not to lead a small group is a natural outgrowth of the training course.

Now we come to the term *potential* in terms of the small-group leader. This term is consistently used in this handbook for several reasons. Because so few church members have enough experience, training, or confidence to lead effective small groups, a church's pool of small-group leaders is typically small. Rare indeed is the church with enough small-group leaders in place to staff a congregation-wide small-group program.

Because we typically have a deficit talent bank when it comes to small-group leaders, we would normally expect to get little response to recruiting efforts. Who would want to accept a leadership position for which she was inadequately prepared? More important, what church can in good conscience call forth people to assume leadership if the necessary leadership gifts are not present? This typical picture may seem bleak or even hopeless. Fortunately, however, most churches probably have more than enough *potential* small-group leaders among their members. All that is lacking, then, is for you to call them forth and train them.

The remainder of this chapter examines this recruiting process while chapter 5 tells you how to plan a leadership training course for your potential small-group leaders.

Because the task of recruiting potential small-group leaders is similar to recruiting church officers, your steering committee's recruitment process is like that of a church's nominating committee.

First, list qualities or characteristics for prospective nominees.

Then use these criteria to select possible candidates.

Finally, ask an adequate number of potential small-group leaders to consider this calling.

Let's turn, then, to each of these steps and examine in detail the recruitment process of prospective small-group leaders.

Listing Qualities of Small-Group Leaders

While you can find the necessary qualities or requirements for church officers in a church's constitution or by-laws, you'll probably have to develop a list of desirable qualities for small-group leaders. As with the creation of other elements in the planning process (such as purpose, goals, and strategy), ask steering committee members to brainstorm and generate a list of desirable qualities for effective small-group leaders.

Here is a list one church developed. The effective small-group leader:

- Is open to others and willing to share self
- Accepts others; is nonjudgmental
- Is willing and able to take initiative
- Is a good listener
- Is a growing person
- Is warm and supportive
- Has confidence in groups
- Has a healthy commitment to Jesus Christ
- Is committed to the church.

As is the case for church officers, you probably won't find many people that possess all desired qualities. Generally speaking, look for people who have healthy, effective interpersonal relations. A list of qualities such as the example above can serve as a guideline to discover people who have or who are likely to develop such characteristics. It is probably unwise to nominate someone who is perceived negatively on any of the qualities on your list. For example, someone who is typically judgmental in interpersonal relations will probably have a difficult time leading an effective group with or without training. Moreover, someone whose faith commitment is antagonistic to Christian beliefs or who is a disgruntled, inactive member is unlikely to have a satisfying group leadership experience. Once your steering committee reaches a consensus on the qualities it desires in its potential small-group leaders, it is ready to assemble and prioritize a list of prospects.

Discovering Prospective Small-Group Leaders

A number of people who possess qualities for effective group leadership may not consider themselves or have been considered by others to be "leaders." Remember, what you seek are people who fit the qualities of a *potential* small-group leader.

To discover candidates for leading small groups, turn to your church's membership directory. This helps your committee to consider everyone in the congregation—not just those who come to mind or who are already serving in other leadership positions.

Again, at first ask committee members to work alone, generating a list of leader candidates. Then the committee can compare notes and decide whom to ask to consider this ministry. A good way to achieve consensus is to list everyone's candidates on a blackboard or newsprint. Then discuss each candidate's qualifications for leading a small group.

Remind folks that this is a call process, not a popularity contest. Neither neglect anyone whose name appears nor discontinue consideration of anyone on any grounds other than that the person does not fit the adopted qualities for effective group leaders. Let people decide for themselves whether or not they wish to participate in the leadership training course; do not exclude any "qualified" prospects from your "to be contacted about training" list. There may be one exception to this rule—if there are too many qualified candidates. If this happens, prioritize your list, taking into account the type of balance desired among your small-group leaders. Such factors might include gender, ethnicity, age, disability, marital status, level of involvement, years of membership, and faith development. In any event, take great care to ensure that the people you select represent your church's diversity. Overlook no group in the church for leadership in your small-group ministry.

Contacting Prospective Small-Group Leaders

The number of people you should contact depends on the number of new groups you project. For example, the 250-member church that wrote the first purpose statement presented in chapter 3 asked fifteen people to participate in its training course. This included all its qualified prospective leaders, enough to lead the ten to fifteen new groups it projected. The 1,200-member congregation, which wrote the second purpose statement, generated an initial list of some 120 qualified potential leaders. Because its steering committee expected many people on the list not to participate, it contacted all 120 prospects, calculating that they would train enough people to lead the projected forty or fifty new small groups. In both instances, the number of desired new groups was based on the expectation that one-third to one-half of their members would join a small-group ministry in its first phase of expansion. In my experience this expectation is realistic.

What if the number of new groups you project is greater than your number of qualified prospective leaders? In such a case I suggest you lower the number of projected new groups. Unqualified prospective leaders are likely to become ineffective group leaders, resulting in frustration for everyone involved. Your congregation must be realistic enough to work within its gifts and resources. If you find yourself in this situation, foster the notion that "small is beautiful"; to do otherwise for the sake of some artificial numbers game could well prove detrimental to your church's ministry.

Who should contact potential small-group leaders? In short, whoever is most likely to get a candidate to give serious consideration to the call. In the 250-member church referred to earlier, many seemed reluctant to become involved. In this instance, the pastor did all the contacting in the hope that people would take this call more seriously than they might if a layperson or other staff member had called. This strategy seemed warranted because in the end nearly all people did decide to participate. In the larger church, two lay steering committee members, one clergy committee member, and three additional clergy staff members shared equally in making the 120 contacts. These contacts yielded the desired forty to fifty prospective leaders.

How should you contact prospective leaders? Either face to face or by telephone. Clearly and succinctly summarize the leadership qualities you see in the person and the commitment you seek (participation in a potential small-group leader training course, followed by consideration of leading or not leading a group). Here are suggestions for an actual phone conversation:

Opening pleasantries . . .

I'm calling on behalf of our church's small-group steering committee. The fellowship committee recently formed our steering committee to expand our church's small-group ministry. This fall we'll be offering training for new small-group leaders. We expect to begin new small groups just after the first of next year. As we thought about members of our church who might be good small-group leaders, your name came up.

We thought of you because of your . . . *(refer to the qualities you see, such as openness to others, warmth and supportiveness).* Our seven-week training course is set for Thursday evenings, late October through mid-December. We hope you will consider taking this course.

After the training, if you'd like to lead a group, that's fine; if not, that's fine too. We think the training will be useful to you no matter when or where you might make use of it.

What do you think? Do you have any questions? Take some time to think and pray about this if you'd like. Let's be in touch by next Wednesday for your decision.

While your leadership recruitment is underway, you can take the next step to expand your small-group ministry: the planning and adoption of a leadership training course.

CHAPTER 5

Planning a Leadership Training Course

What factors should you consider when you plan your leadership training course? I recommend these five: (1) purpose, (2) duration, (3) methods, (4) topics, and (5) trainer. Let's examine each of these.

Purpose

Simply put, a small-group leadership training course should provide the theory, experience, and practice for your participants to gain the knowledge and skills they'll need to become effective leaders of small groups. I find that it works best to gear the course for people who have little group leadership training or experience but who are willing to *consider* leading a small group. While it is unrealistic for you to expect highly refined skills to result from your training course, participants can gain enough knowledge and skills to acquire the basic confidence and competence needed to begin leading an effective group. A course offers necessary background allowing participants to become skillful leaders as they gain experience in the coming years.

Duration

A six- to ten-week course with two- to three-hour sessions (twelve to thirty total hours) is adequate for most effective small-group leadership training courses. Your course needs to be long enough for you to cover all basic topics and skills but not so long that it deters prospective leaders from taking the course. Because most laypeople are used to meeting once a week for classes in the church, a once-per-week format is probably easiest to arrange. A workshop approach, scheduling several one- or two-day blocks of time, is another possibility, as is a combination of scheduling formats. Schedule adequate time to cover all essential topics; allow time for your participants to complete necessary assignments between sessions.

Methods

Let your training methods fit the topics you cover and the outcome you seek. A variety of teaching methods best serve the variety of topics I suggest you cover. (See chapter 6.) You can best accomplish some learning goals by emphasizing theory; others are best taught as they are modeled by the trainer and thereby experienced; still others through practice.

And remember that people of differing temperaments and ways of perceiving best learn in differing ways.

For these reasons consider a variety of training methods, including a theoretical approach with lecture-discussions to teach about leading; an experiential approach in which group leadership is modeled by the trainer; and a practical approach with hands-on activities to learn by doing.

Topics

To provide opportunity for your participants to acquire the basic knowledge and skills to become effective leaders of small groups, include a number of topics. The following topics are detailed more fully in chapter 6:

*   An introduction to leading small groups in the church; include an overview of creating Christian community through small groups; examine participants' leadership style and behavior.
*   How to lead group sharing—building a supportive climate and facilitating member participation.
*   How to lead group study—forming and using discussion questions, and choosing study resources.

- How to lead group prayer—conversational prayer.
- How to lead group mission—balancing group life and group task.
- How to start small groups —forming new groups and handling difficulties.

Leading Small Groups in the Church: A Training Course Description

The following training course description illustrates how *purpose, duration, methods*, and *topics* relate to one another.

Purpose

To provide necessary theory, experience, and practice to gain the basic knowledge and skills to become an effective small-group leader.

Participants

This course is for people who may have little small-group leadership training or experience but who are willing to consider leading a small group. Qualities such as openness, acceptance, warmth, and growth in interpersonal relations are especially important for prospective small-group leaders.

Time

Arranged according to participant goals and schedules. The course lasts from six to ten weeks with two- to three-hour sessions (twelve to thirty total hours).

Methods

A variety of training methods will be used, including a theoretical approach (with lecture-discussion to learn about leading), an experiential approach (with trainer-led activities to learn through experience), and a practical approach (with hands-on activities to learn by doing). The trainer will match the most suitable approach with particular learning goals and participant learning styles.

Course Outline

The following schedule outlines a ten-week course, focusing on the use of the three training methods. Note that the detailed training outline presented in chapter 6 is for a seven-week course.

Topics	Training Methods (Two-Hour Sessions)		
	Theory	Experience	Practice
I. INTRODUCTION TO SMALL GROUPS IN THE CHURCH (two sessions)			
Week 1			
A. Creating Community	1/2 hr.	1/2 hr.	
B. Significant Observations on Small Groups in the Church	1/2 hr.	1/2 hr.	
Week 2			
C. Assessing Leadership Styles and Behaviors	1 hr.	1 hr.	

(schedule continues)

Topics	Training Methods (Two-Hour Sessions)		
	Theory	Experience	Practice

II. AREAS OF GROUP LIFE
(six sessions)

Weeks 3 and 4
A. Leading Group Sharing

- Building a Supportive Climate	1/2 hr.	1/2 hr.	1 hr.
- Facilitating Member Participation	1/2 hr.	1/2 hr.	1 hr.

Weeks 5, 6, 7, and 8
B. Leading Group Study

- Forming and Using Discussion Questions	1 hr.	1 hr.	2 hrs.
- Choosing Study Resources	1/2 hr.		1/2 hr.

C. Leading Group Prayer

- Developing Conversational Prayer	1/2 hr.	1/2 hr.	1/2 hr.

D. Leading Group Mission

- Balancing the Inward and Outward Journey	1/2 hr.		
- Establishing a Group Task	1/2 hr.		1/2 hr.

III. STARTING SMALL GROUPS
(two sessions)

Weeks 9 and 10

A. Forming New Groups	1/2 hr.	1/2 hr.	1/2 hr.
B. Creating Group Purposes and Agreements	1/2 hr.		1/2 hr.
C. Initiating a Group and Handling Difficulties	1/2 hr.		1/2 hr.
D. Supporting Group Leaders	1/2 hr.		

TOTAL (ten sessions)	8 hrs.	5 hrs.	7 hrs.

Trainer

In all likelihood you will have a hard time finding a qualified small-
group leadership trainer. Remember the reason more of our churches do
not have a small-group ministry: So few of our churches know how to
do the necessary planning or training. The training of small-group ministry planners and trainers is typically not part of the curriculum in most of
our theological seminaries. If you seek the services of small-group communication consultants or academicians, you'll find that many do not
have the background, experience, or interest in training volunteer leaders
in general or church leaders in particular. Indeed, obtaining the services
of a trainer for your prospective leaders may be a most disconcerting and
frustrating problem for your steering committee. This handbook is writ-
ten precisely to help churches solve this problem.

    It is my hope and expectation that you will find in this handbook all
the ideas and resources you need to plan a ministry and train leaders to
assist your church in creating Christian community through small groups.
In the next section you will find a suggested curriculum for a training
course.

The Training

CHAPTER 6

Training Potential Small-Group Leaders

Besides good planning, nothing is more important for developing an effective small-group ministry than good leadership training. Without proper attention to the training of potential small-group leaders, it is unlikely that your program will be effective in creating Christian community.

This chapter is a ready-to-use trainer's guide complete with topics, learning objectives, teaching resources and strategies, and assignments for a typical small-group leadership training course.

Though this chapter is addressed to trainers, each participant should have access to a copy of this book to complete homework assignments.

The outline on page 54 lays out a seven-week course you can follow to train your prospective small-group leaders. While you can surely offer shorter (four-session) or longer (ten-session) versions of the course, I think you'll find that the following seven-week course provides adequate coverage of basic knowledge and skills within scheduling constraints placed on most churches and participants.

For a ten-session schedule, see the end of chapter 5.

In a four-session course, cover the first four units presented. (Omit unit 5.) Within the four units, cover the topics marked with asterisks. Later on, if leaders discover they need help in areas not covered in the four-week course, try to schedule additional training.

Each week is planned for a two-hour period. Allow five to ten minutes of start-up and wrap-up time and take a ten-minute coffee break. This gives you ninety to one hundred minutes of actual training time.

Here, then, is our seven-week training course outline:

Seven-Week Course Outline

UNIT 1: Leading Small Groups in the Church: Introduction

Week 1
- Creating Christian Community through Small Groups in the Church*
- Assessing Leadership Style and Behavior*

UNIT 2: Leading Group Sharing

Week 2
- Introduction and Review*
- Building a Supportive Climate*

Week 3
- Review
- Facilitating Member Participation

UNIT 3: Leading Group Study

Week 4
- Introduction and Review*
- Forming and Using Discussion Questions*

Week 5
- Review
- Choosing Study Resources

UNIT 4: Leading Group Prayer and Mission

Week 6
- Developing Conversational Prayer*
- Balancing Group Life and Group Task*

UNIT 5: Starting Small Groups

Week 7
- Introduction
- Forming New Groups
- Handling Difficulties

Unit 1:
Leading Small Groups in the Church: Introduction

(Week 1)

Learning Objectives

1. To acquaint participants with the value, nature, function, and leadership of small groups in the church, so that they have an overall picture of how Christian community develops in a congregation.

2. To examine what makes small-group leaders effective and in-effective, including the assessment of leadership style and behavior, so that participants can identify the strengths and potential of their group-leadership skills.

Topic 1: Creating Christian Community through Small Groups in the Church

Resources

A. "The Role of Small Groups in Creating Christian Community," from chapter 2.

B. "Some Significant Observations on Small Groups in the Church," from chapter 2.

Strategies

"The Role of Small Groups" and "Some Significant Observations" from chapter 2 provide a good overview of the value, nature, function, and leadership of small groups in the church.

A. First, summarize "The Role of Small Groups" to introduce your leadership training course.

B. Divide participants into groups of three to five. Have them get acquainted by telling one another one or two of their own "significant observations" about small groups in the church.

C. Reconvene the whole group and have each small group report one or two observations or "learnings" per group. Following this exchange, contribute your own personal observations and highlight excerpts from "Some Significant Observations" in chapter 2. At this point, your participants should have a clear picture of how Christian community can develop through a small-group ministry. (Spend about 45 minutes on topic 1.)

Topic 2: Assessing Leadership Style and Behavior

Resources

A. "An Overview of Effective Small-Group Leadership." See appendix Λ.

B. "Leadership Style Inventory." See appendix B.

C. "Characteristics of Effective and Ineffective Small-Group Discussion Leaders." See appendix C.

Strategies

A. Ask participants what they think makes a small-group leader effective. Then summarize and discuss the research findings on this topic from appendix A. (Take 15-20 minutes.)

B. Assess and interpret participants' leadership styles using the inventory found in appendix B. (Take 15-20 minutes.)

C. Refer your participants to the list of characteristics of effective and ineffective small-group discussion leaders in appendix C. Have them select specific task and/or relationship behaviors to develop and to avoid. (In unit 2 [week 2] we will work on developing flexibility in leadership style.) (Take 15-20 minutes.)

Assignments

As preparation for unit 2, ask participants to review "Some Significant Observations" found in chapter 2.

Unit 2:
Leading Group Sharing

(Weeks 2 and 3)

Overview

In a seven-week course this unit would be covered in two different sessions. (Omit the week-3 session in a shortened four-week version of the course.) A week-2 session should introduce the unit and teach ways in which leaders can foster an atmosphere of openness and acceptance in a small group.

Week 3 should review week 2 and focus on the very important yet seldom studied area of how leaders can facilitate the involvement of all members in group interaction.

Learning Objectives

1. To present and demonstrate resources participants can use to begin building a supportive atmosphere in a group.

2. To provide opportunities for participants to practice the building of a supportive climate in a group.

3. To provide opportunities for participants to work at developing leadership behaviors identified in unit 1 that can enable them to become effective, adaptable leaders.

4. To present suggestions for facilitating member participation so that participants can identify specific strengths and areas to improve. (Omit in a four-week course.)

5. To provide opportunities for participants to improve their ability to facilitate member participation. (Omit in a four-week course.)

Week 2: Building a Supportive Climate

Topic 1: Introduction and Review

Two important assumptions about leading small groups (previously mentioned in "Some Significant Observations" from chapter 2) need further explanation. One assumption concerns the definition of a leader while the other assumption concerns the level of competence needed to lead effective groups. Discuss these assumptions with your participants. (Take 15-20 minutes.)

   A. *Definition of a leader.* While leadership may emerge naturally in some groups, most groups in the church have a leader—a member of the group designated to help the group accomplish its task and work as a team. In short, *a leader is a member of the group who helps the group go where it wants to go to the extent that such help is needed.*[1]
   This definition views leadership on a sliding scale in which the leader's task may be large or small, depending on the group's need for direction and facilitation. Early in the group's life, the designated leader can be especially helpful in assisting the group to establish its purpose and agreements, in building a supportive group climate, and in making suggestions for member participation. In ongoing group life, the leader's main task is to facilitate member participation so that the group can accomplish its purposes. One person may provide this leadership—the designated leader—or several members may share it. Ideally, other group members will soon share in moving the group along in its task and relational dimensions.

   B. *Level of competence.* How many group activities should we prepare our leaders to lead? While many groups start with one focus, say study or prayer, they frequently take on other group activities such as sharing or mission. This means group leaders must be able to lead the primary activities of group life. Four such activities are sharing, study, prayer, and mission. Other activities could include celebration and growth. Because sharing, study, prayer, and mission are the most common primary activities of most of our church groups, we'll look at each of these activities, beginning with leading group sharing and the building of a supportive climate.

Topic 2: Building a Supportive Climate

Resources

A. "Developing a Supportive Climate." See appendix D.

B. "Sharing Questions." See appendix E.

Strategies

A. Begin topic 2 with a lecture-discussion on the *theory* of developing a supportive group climate. Use the material in appendix D. (Take 15 minutes.)

B. To allow participants to *experience* the building of a supportive climate, divide them into groups of three or four. Have them get acquainted with one another using questions 1 and 24 from the first list in appendix E.

C. After fifteen or twenty minutes (whenever the groups finish this exercise), have participants continue experiencing the building of a supportive climate in their groups by asking them to select more "sharing questions" to discuss among themselves. They can select questions from the lists in appendix E or make up their own. Shift responsibility for group direction to group members, beginning the *practice* of leading group sharing.

Have participants take turns leading the small group using questions of their choice. Moderate this round of practice by having the responsibility for group direction rotate from one group member to the next every five or six minutes. (Take 15-20 minutes total.)

D. Following the initial round of practice in leading group sharing, add another training dimension: development of leadership style flexibility. Ask participants to recall the specific task and/or relationship behaviors they selected from the "Characteristics of Effective and Ineffective Small-Group Discussion Leaders" list. To help participants expand their repertory of leadership behaviors and develop flexibility in their leadership style, have them choose one or two specific behaviors on which to work as they take their next turns of leading group sharing. Moderate another fifteen- to twenty-minute practice round or two.

E. Close this practice session by asking participants to discuss their progress with their group. Then reconvene the whole group for a short debriefing session on using "sharing questions" to build a supportive group climate. (Take 10 minutes.)

Your participants will get more practice in leading group sharing and developing a flexible leadership style in the session that follows: "Facilitating Member Participation." (Omit in a four-week course.)

Assignments (Omit in a four-week course.)

To prepare for the week-3 session, have participants complete the very last "spiritual" question in appendix E ("life-story") and select two or three additional "sharing questions" that interest them. These additional questions might come from the lists in appendix E. But encourage participants to make up their own questions so they can experience the creative process they'll use to come up with questions in the future.

Week 3: Facilitating Member Participation
(Omit in a four-week course.)

Topic 1: Review and Introduction

Strategies

A. As a transition between the session on building a supportive climate and this session on facilitating member participation, ask participants to form the same small groups (of three or four) they were in last week. (This continuation allows participants to *experience* the development of a supportive climate just as it would normally occur in early group life; to *experience* the unique way the life-story "sharing question" enhances group cohesion; to *practice* the leading of group sharing; and to develop a flexible leadership style.)

B. Ask participants to tell their small groups their "life stories." Have group members talk about one stage of their lives or perhaps one or two main life-influences. (There will not be time for participants to share all parts of their life-stories.) After everyone takes five minutes to tell a life-story, have participants continue sharing using the additional questions they selected for homework. (Take 45 minutes in all.) This exercise gives people an idea of how to use this method of group sharing and of how valuable it is for building a supportive atmosphere in a group.

Moderate group leadership as you did in the last session. Rotate group leadership among group members but give each person ten minutes per turn. This allows participants to log more practice in leading group sharing and using the task and/or relationship behaviors they've selected to develop flexibility in their leadership styles.

After each group member has had one or two more turns leading the group, the first three objectives of unit 2 should be fairly well met.

Topic 2: Facilitating Member Participation

Resources

A. "Suggestions for Facilitating Member Participation." See appendix F.

Strategies

A. While work can continue on experiencing a supportive climate and practicing leadership skills and flexibility of leadership style, we turn our attention to learning objectives 4 and 5.

Participants can reach these learning objectives—focused on facilitating member participation—in the context of ongoing group life. Point out this fact so participants realize that many of the dynamics of group life and leadership they experience in the training session are likely to occur in groups they eventually lead.

B. Present and discuss the sixteen suggestions for facilitating member participation listed in appendix F.2 While these suggestions are directed toward discussion-group members, they are relevant for most church small groups, whether a group's focus is on sharing, study, prayer, or mission; whatever activity or activities a group chooses for its center, group discussion will ordinarily be a prominent part of the group's life. These suggestions are also relevant for our participants in their dual roles as members and leaders. Remember, we're training leaders who are group members as well as members who help facilitate group interaction. Participants can work to strengthen their own group participation even as they facilitate others' member behavior; they can do so whether or not they are functioning as their group's "designated leader."

C. Ask all participants to select one or two items from appendix F that best describe their membership behavior and one or two suggestions that they could heed to be a better group participant. Now they are ready to work on strengthening their own participation as a group member.

D. To practice and improve facilitation skills, have all members tell their small group which specific participation behaviors they are trying to improve. This way, group members can work at facilitating member participation and improving their own group participation at the same time.

E. Have group leaders use a "sharing question" already "on the table" or switch to another question of their choice. Another round or two of such group leadership (rotating leaders every ten minutes or so) should allow ample time for everyone to make satisfactory progress at improving (1) their leadership of group sharing—covered in week 2, (2) their facilitation of member participation, and (3) their own group participation. (Take about 45 minutes.)

F. Following this practice, take five minutes and have participants debrief their experience. Be sure to include a chance for members to give feedback to one another regarding the progress they've made.

G. Finally, close this training session with a five- to ten-minute plenary group discussion in which your participants report insights they've gained about facilitating member participation, specifically, and leading group sharing, generally.

Assignments

As preparation for unit 3 (week 4), ask participants to formulate three to six discussion questions that can stimulate group discussion for a particular scripture passage (for example, Luke 19:1-9 or 10). Have everyone use the same passage. You might introduce this assignment by giving a five- to ten-minute overview of how to form discussion questions (see appendix G). On the other hand, there may be value in having participants generate discussion questions on their own prior to your presentation. Have your participants make this decision based on whether they feel they need suggestions for generating discussion questions.

Unit 3:
Leading Group Study

(Weeks 4 and 5)

Overview

This training unit focuses on the leading of study in a group. As in prior training units, use theoretical, experiential, and practical teaching strategies where most applicable in meeting the unit's learning objectives. This unit includes two training sessions.

Learning Objectives

1. To acquaint participants with principles of how to form discussion questions so that they are able to recognize and generate questions that stimulate good discussion of study materials.

2. To provide practice forming and using discussion questions so that participants can develop basic skills and confidence in leading group study.

3. To acquaint participants with various types of study resources that are available for use by small groups in the church, including criteria for choosing study materials that create a sense of community in study groups. (Omit in a four-week course.)

Week 4: Forming and Using Discussion Questions

Topic 1. Introduction

As with leading other group activities, the purpose of leading group study is to further the development of a sense of Christian community. While small groups can be *part* of a church's life and mission (that is, a vehicle for Christian formation), they can also be at the *heart* of a congregation's life and mission. While the former use of groups—as solely a medium for growth and learning—is surely valid, the latter is the focus of this handbook and training course.

Remind participants that study should bring Life to group members so that they may bring Life to people outside the group. Remind them that a sense of community is centered in *sharing something with someone*. Whether this sharing involves study, support, prayer, or mission, a group should be both an end in itself as well as a means to an end. A group meeting in Christ's name should bring acceptance, openness, support, and growth to group members so that they are able to experience Life as it was intended to be lived. But to hold on to Life without offering it to others denies the covenant nature of Christian living—our experiencing Life in order that others might also experience Life. So remind participants that small groups that study (or share or pray or serve) but do not lead to the experience of Life among group members *and* for those beyond the group are not really small groups that bring a sense of Christian community in a congregation. Unless their sole purpose is for growth and learning (Christian formation), they are groups that become either so turned in upon themselves that they forget those beyond the group or so other-directed that they forget those within the group.

The focus of this training unit, then, is the activity of study as a vehicle for building a sense of community among congregational members. Let's look at the leading of such study.

Topic 2. Forming and Using Discussion Questions

Resources

A. "The Inductive Method of Group Discussion." See appendix G.

B. "The Relational Method of Study" (outlined below).
(Omit in a four-week course.)

Strategies

A. If you did not present a five- to ten-minute overview of the inductive method of study (see appendix G) at the conclusion of the week-3 session, present the theory here.

B. So that your participants may experience the inductive method of study in action, lead an abbreviated fifteen- to twenty-minute plenary discussion using the Leslie excerpt and the discussion questions in appendix G.

C. Follow up with a ten- to fifteen-minute discussion on how the questions were formed and used. From this demonstration and discussion, several *principles* of creating and using discussion questions usually surface, including:

- Questions should be open-ended rather than calling for yes-no answers.

- Questions should allow for more than one answer, not just the leader's answer.

- Questions should require study of the material at hand and keep discussion focused on the material rather than foster speculative reports based on outside experts.

- While it is preferable to use questions in an orderly fashion (observation questions first, followed by questions of interpretation and application, respectively), the spontaneity characteristic of many good discussions may require flexibility in the use of questions.

- Questions need not be asked if the areas to which they relate have already been adequately covered in group discussion.

- Back-up questions may be needed to cover a topic area adequately or to focus discussion effectively.

- Groups frequently move to the interpretation-level of inquiry before enough observations are made. When this happens, it may be necessary to return to the observation level.

- Application questions are frequently difficult to form and usually require the most creativity.

- Unplanned areas of group inquiry should be encouraged if they are relevant to the material being studied.

- Leaders should remember that planned questions are simply aids to stimulate discussion so that a group can better understand and apply the material.

D. Your participants should be ready to *practice* the formation and use of effective inductive study questions. Participants can get good practice in creating discussion questions by working individually to improve the questions they brought with them to the training session. (Take 5-10 minutes.)

E. In addition to individual work at improving their questions, have people return to their original groups of three or four and work together to create a complete set of inductive study questions for the passage of material you assigned as homework. You can act as a resource during this phase. (Take 10-15 minutes.)

F. Finally, close this session with participants taking turns leading a forty- to fifty-minute group study using the inductive study questions they created together. Each group member can practice leading group study for five to ten minutes at a time until the group completes the study. (If time permits, have each group briefly report how well their discussion questions worked.)

Assignments
(Omit in a four-week course.)

Give two assignments for participants to complete before the second session of the "Leading Group Study" unit (week 5):

A. Form five or six inductive study questions for a passage selected by the small group. (Each person in a small group should work on the same passage.)

B. Bring group study resource materials such as those listed in appendix H for everyone to examine. Materials might be those that will help in leading discussion or matierals "worthy" of discussion.

Week 5: Choosing Study Resources
(Omit in a four-week course.)

Topic 1: Review and Introduction

Strategies

A. Devote most of this session to more practice of forming and
using inductive study questions. Have participants meet again in the
same small groups and compare and contrast the questions they prepared
for the passage their group selected to study. Ask them to work together
to shape discussion questions, perhaps arriving at a consensus for questions at each level of inquiry. (Take 15-20 minutes.)

B. Have each group use these questions to study their passage;
havee leadership rotate among group members as in previous practice
sessions. Group members may now want more time for leading their
group, perhaps ten to twenty minutes per member. Let group leadership
rotate among members until they finish their study, probably forty-five
to sixty minutes in all.

C. Another debriefing session either in small groups or in plenary
discussion can provide fitting closure to this part of the training session.

D. *Alternate option:* An alternate focus for this second session
on leading group study is the relational method of study suggested by
Leslie.[3] In fact, your groups can use the study Leslie outlines for Luke
19:1-9 or 10:

a. Read the Scripture reference out loud using different voices
for different characters where applicable and using modern transla-
tions freely.

b. Discuss the associations stirred in your mind by this passage.
You are an expert on what associations come to your mind. Share
these associations in as personal a way as you can.

c. What do you think this story is really about in terms of a
timeless, interpersonal incident?

d. Have you ever been "up a tree" like Zacchaeus? When have you felt cut off?

e. When you felt cut off, what helped?

f. Discuss the meaning of salvation in Luke 19:9.

(Reprinted from Robert Leslie, *Sharing Groups in the Church* [Nashville: Abingdon, 1971], 40-42.)

Another relational Bible study resource is *The NIV Serendipity Bible Study Book*.[4] You might have participants compare the Leslie and *Serendipity* questions for a certain passage, possibly Luke 19.

E. If participants seek more information on leading effective group discussions, refer them to other publications.[5]

Now that you have devoted one and two-thirds sessions to the first two learning objectives of unit 3, it is time to examine selected resources for group study and meet objective 3.

Topic 2: Choosing Study Resources

Resources

"Selected Study Resources." See appendix H.

Strategies

A. At the beginning of the session, display in relevant categories the study materials participants brought with them to this session. See appendix H for sample categories and representative study resource materials.

B. After members look over the study materials (perhaps during a coffee break), lead a plenary discussion about how to choose study resources. (Take 30 minutes.)

Point out that the primary criterion for selecting study resources is to have them fit the group's purpose. Groups must know the reason they want to study and decide the type of study they prefer. Also, groups must determine how their study will foster the creation of Christian community.

Point out that discussion guides are available for some studies while group discussion questions need to be created for other studies. The study resources that people bring with them as well as those listed in appendix H represent, of course, only a fraction of available study materials. Frequently groups are unaware of the rich variety of resource material available for them to study, so group leaders can provide a very valuable service by calling the group's attention to study material options. Church and denominational staff are often valuable reference people for finding fitting study materials.

Assignments
(Optional)

An optional assignment is to ask if anyone wishes to prepare and be ready (at the end of session 6 or in session 7) to deliver a brief, informational report on various types of groups or activities you did not include in the training course. Reports might be in the form of three- or four-minute "book reports" of the following resources:

- Walt Marcum, *Sharing Groups in Youth Ministry* (Abingdon, 1991).

- Howard Clinebell, *Growth Groups* (Abingdon, 1977).

- Howard Kirschenbaum and Barbara Glaser, *Developing Support Groups* (University Associates, 1978).

- Clyde Reid, *Celebrate the Temporary* (Harper & Row, 1972).

- Warren Hartman, *Five Audiences* (Abingdon, 1989) offers exceedingly helpful insights for forming groups around people's interests and expectations rather than around their gender, age, or marital status.

- William Clemmons and Harvey Nestor, *Growth through Groups* (Broadman, 1974) describe how personal and congregational growth can happen through small groups in the areas of koinonia (fellowship), personal Christian depth, and mission.

Unit 4:
Leading Group Prayer and Mission

(Week 6)

Overview

I treat these two topics, prayer and mission, together in one unit not because they are of lesser importance than the activities of sharing and study. It is simply that the ideas to present and skills to develop for these areas are fewer than for leading group sharing and study. Normally, then, you can cover the leading of these two group activities in one training session. We'll consider the leading of each activity in turn—first leading group prayer, and then leading group mission.

Learning Objectives

1. To expose participants to the concept of conversational prayer so that they come to see its value and naturalness in group life.

2. To provide opportunity for participants to experience conversational prayer and to practice leading it.

3. To discuss the relationship between Christian life and Christian service so that participants realize that fellowship and mission are indispensable parts of authentic Christian community.

4. To examine how to form and develop mission groups so participants learn what it takes to lead such groups.

Topic 1: Leading Group Prayer

Strategies

A. A stimulating way to begin this session is to ask your participants to share their experiences with prayer in the church and/or prayer in church groups. (Take 5-10 minutes.)

Or you might begin in groups, asking participants to share briefly their expectations about the session and/or one or two important things about their lives during the past week. Then have them pray for one another in sentence prayers about the expectations and/or things they share.

In either case, your participants may report feeling uncomfortable, awkward, or uneasy about their experiences with group prayer. Several will no doubt say something like "I feel I have to pray in a certain way"; "My heart beats rapidly and I feel like I have a lump in my throat right before I pray"; "I feel dumb when I pray because I don't do it very well"; "I'm just not comfortable praying out loud in a group—that's for 'spiritual people' like the pastor"; or "I can never think of anything important to say, at least nothing that's long enough for a prayer."

B. As an alternative to the type of prayer with which many of your participants may be familiar, introduce the notion of conversational prayer. (Take 10 minutes.)

Suggest that, like a conversation, prayer can be:

- Informal and voluntary rather than formal or obligatory.

- Genuine and light-hearted rather than phony or stuffy.

- Free-flowing and focused rather than mechanical or disjointed.

- Spontaneous and natural rather than forced or contrived.

- Brief and to the point rather than lengthy or compulsive.

- Interpersonal and involved rather than private or detached.

Conversational prayer is an experience of relating together with one another and with God present there in the group; it is not a performance before an audience with God listening in from afar. So group members can be themselves, can speak in a natural, spontaneous manner, and can take turns praying together about whatever topics emerge to a God who is present, who cares about their lives, and who eagerly and sympathetically responds to their concerns. Group members who talk with one another and God this way about things that matter most can expect to experience changes that improve the everyday condition of their lives and relationships—both in mundane and extraordinary matters.6

C. After your participants hear *about* conversational prayer as an alternative to the typical group prayer to which many are accustomed, have them move back to their original groups to *experience* conversational prayer.

Encourage your group members to share with one another some things they consider important about the training session and/or their lives. Then invite one member of each group to begin with a personal, direct, sentence-length prayer about something someone in the group just said. Encourage other members to join in and talk with one another and God about this subject until it seems complete. Someone can then simply move the group to a new subject of conversational prayer with others joining in as they desire. While all members will not, of course, pray about each topic, encourage everyone to take several turns, contributing something to the prayer conversation. (Take 5-15 minutes.)

D. Have group members discuss how their experience of conversational prayer went. (Take 5-10 minutes.)

E. Following the debriefing experience, consider two final aspects of this group activity: (1) the contribution prayer makes in group life and (2) the leadership conversational prayer requires. (Take 10 minutes.)

(1) Stress the importance of groups deciding the contribution prayer will make in their life together. What role will prayer play in the group's life? Some groups may decide to make prayer their primary activity. On the other hand, prayer may not be prominent at all or it may be a secondary activity. If prayer is chosen as a group activity, the group needs to decide carefully the purpose, function, and method of prayer. Once these decisions are made, the matter of leading group prayer is quite straightforward.

(2) The primary task of leading group prayer is to facilitate or coordinate the process of praying. Early in group life the leader might want to suggest that the group focus on certain types of prayer (e.g., thanksgiving, confession, intercession) and on various topics (the world, the church, friends and relatives). As the group establishes its prayer life, it will probably need very little group direction and may find its members freely sharing the prayer leadership.

F. *Note:* Participants will receive more practice leading conversational prayer at the conclusion of this training session, following your presentation of topic 2.

Topic 2: Balancing Group Life and Group Task

Strategies

A. A good introduction to topic 2 is the following reference to Elizabeth O'Connor's *Journey Inward, Journey Outward,* made Robert Leslie: "Effective groups are neither exclusively person-oriented nor exclusively task-oriented but combine features of both emphases. The 'journey inward' is complemented by the 'journey outward' and vice-versa. 'Talking groups' are not enough where 'action' groups are called for."[7]

B. Point out that the relationship between our life together inside the group and our life outside the group is very much like the relationship between our congregation's life and service; both are essential parts of the whole. As O'Connor suggests, members have both a life in the group and a life beyond the group. While this journey inward and outward is characteristic of all effective groups, the leader must consider the issue of emphasis: In this group, which journey is predominant?

Some groups may emphasize inward-journey activities (sharing, study, prayer, etc.), while others may center on outward-journey activities (mission). Even as every group has both its own life and a life beyond the group, so each group may emphasize one or the other. Both are necessary for effective group life even though one may be more prominent. Some groups, then, may choose to emphasize group mission and focus primarily on reaching out in service to those beyond the group. Yet without adequate attention to the inward journey of support and care for one another, group members will not be able to sustain their service to those beyond the group.[8]

Likewise, groups that emphasize sharing, study, or prayer and offer support of members' lives but have no impact on members' service to those beyond the group can become turned in on themselves and die. The purpose of small groups in the church is to provide support for members so that as members live those outside the group may also receive Life. Whether a group emphasizes mission, sharing, study, or prayer, then, it must remind itself that it has both an inner life and an outer life. In short, the key to effective small groups in the church is to *balance* group life and group task.

C. Before turning to the nature and leadership of group mission per se, make one final introductory point regarding the relationship between group life and group task: This point concerns fellowship and evangelism. In an article titled "Fellowship: The Key to Witnessing," Richard Halverson contributes keen insight into the essential connection between congregational life and mission:

> Evangelism was not an issue in the New Testament. The apostles did not urge, exhort, scold, plan and organize evangelistic programs.
>
> In the apostolic church evangelism was somehow assumed, and it functioned without special meetings, special courses, special training, special techniques or special programs.
>
> Evangelism happened! Issuing effortlessly from the community of believers as light does from the sun, evangelism was automatic, spontaneous, continuous and contagious. . . .
>
> Authentic Christian fellowship was the matrix of all New Testament evangelism. Witnessing proceeded out of fellowship and in to fellowship. . . .
>
> In the apostolic church, the relationship between believers and God and between fellow believers was paramount. The forgiving and accepting spirit that emanated from that unique community penetrated a jaded, bored, loveless, weary culture and awakened the spiritual hunger of both Jew and pagan. It was said of them "Lo, how they love one another!" Sin-sick, fed up [people] tried to understand the strange and inviting quality of life that marked the disciples.[9]

If you can find a copy of Halverson's article, it might be valuable for your participants to read and discuss. Its thesis that witness to the gospel arises naturally from Christian community is closely related to balancing group life and group task. We need only recall Jesus' teaching in John 13 and John 15 that the way he wants his disciples to be identified as his disciples is by their love for one another. As I stated in chapter 2, this means that the way Christians treat one another is the witness to the gospel. The quality of Christian "life together" is what draws people to ask: "What's going on here? This Life is attractive and I'd like to experience it too!" This is the place where verbalization of the gospel comes into play: to explain where this attractive quality of life, this authentic Christian community, comes from.

Remind participants, then, that a small-group ministry can be the primary means by which a congregation expresses its life and mission. No matter what activities are prominent in a group, as long as a group balances its group life and its group task, it should *by its very nature* be an "evangelizing fellowship" group.10

D. After your participants see the importance of balancing group life and group task and the overall relationship between mission and other group activities, discuss the nature of mission groups and mission leadership per se.

Point to Cosby's suggestion that mission groups form best around one or two people's interests.11 Once one or two people sense a call to a particular mission area, they invite other members of the congregation to join with them as a mission group.12 If other people join this nucleus, the group develops the support and care necessary to sustain the mission task that emerges in the group.

Consequently, the main duty in leading group mission is to help members develop a supportive, caring group life and clarify the way they'll accomplish their group task. Once the group begins to become a cohesive, supportive unit and decides how it will accomplish its task, the ongoing function of leadership in mission is one of coordination or facilitation to balance group task and group life. (Take 30-45 minutes in lecture-discussion for strategy items A-D.)

E. As closure for training unit 4, have participants return to their established small groups and briefly share their perceptions and expectations about leading group mission. They should do this *in the context of conversational prayer*—talking to God and to one another. As they do this they should take turns leading the group prayer, which should last for a total of five to ten minutes.

F. Time permitting, a final optional activity is to ask participants to expand one another's horizons by making brief informational reports about types of groups and/or group activities that this training has not covered. Your goal here is simply to remind participants as they consider starting small groups that there are other types of groups and group activities than the four covered in this course.

If group leaders start one of the other types of groups, they should find some value in these additional resources. This activity could be carried over to the beginning of next week's class.

Assignments
(Omit in a four-week course.)

A. As preparation for the unit on starting small groups, ask participants to write a paragraph description for the type of small group they would like to lead and/or in which they would like to be a member.

Group descriptions might include group name and activity(ies), quality of group life, group purpose, and practical matters such as meeting time, frequency, and duration. Ask them to bring their descriptions to the next session. If people need more direction or would like an example, read one or two of the group descriptions in chapter 7. Encourage them to work by themselves, using their own creativity, ingenuity, and "voice within."

B. Ask participants to write and bring a list of possible difficulties they foresee in leading a small group in the church (e.g., handling a dominating group member, dealing with frustration, dealing with superficiality and members who avoid depth).

Unit 5
Starting Small Groups

(Week 7)
(Omit this unit in a four-week course.)

Overview

This final training unit covers Forming New Groups and Handling Difficulties. One training session should be adequate to meet the learning objectives of unit 5.

Learning Objectives

1. To have participants gain an overview of the expansion process for a small-group ministry so that they know where the training course fits into overall planning.

2. To have participants share with one another their intentions regarding future group leadership and/or group membership so that (1) the steering committee can proceed with its small-group ministry coordination and interpretation tasks and (2) participants can experience the excitement of seeing direct results from their training efforts.

3. To clarify the necessary steps to start a new small group so that participants who will soon be leading a group know the mechanics of getting a group underway.

4. To discuss difficulties group leaders may encounter so that participants are better prepared to handle them.

Topic 1: Introduction *(optional)*

Complete brief informational book reports not presented or ready at the end of last week's session.

Topic 2: Forming New Groups

Resources

    A. Sections of "Some Significant Observations" from chapter 2.

    B. Steering committee members (outlined below).

    C. Group descriptions (outlined below).

    D. Presentation on "Starting New Groups." See appendix I.

Strategies

    A. Use pertinent sections from "Some Significant Observations on Small Groups in the Church" to give a ten-minute overview of guidelines for forming new groups.

    B. Have members of your small-group ministry steering committee report the plans for expanding your church's small-group ministry. Ask them to speak for about fifteen minutes and clearly explain (1) how the training course fits into the expansion process; (2) that participants are not expected to make a commitment to lead a small group; (3) but that now is the time for participants who would like to lead and/or participate in a small group to make their desire known to the steering committee and to their training-course colleagues.

    C. In a plenary group, take fifteen to twenty minutes for everyone to read aloud the paragraph group-descriptions they wrote as "homework." Participants may experience elation at hearing others declare their interests in leading quite diverse groups.

    D. Collect the paragraph descriptions. (Ask that people put their names on them.) Give them to your steering committee, which can begin its job of coordinating the necessary details to channel this willingness to lead or participate in new small groups. In fact, your steering committee can use the descriptions the training-course participants create as (1) "calls" for new groups; (2) indications of their willingness to lead these new groups; and (3) foci for forming new groups. Some who had been merely potential small-group leaders prior to the training course are now ready and equipped to lead small groups. This is exciting for both your participants and your steering committee members!

E. Thank participants who do not now wish to lead or participate in a new small group for their time and attention. (Keep in touch with them as they may decide to become involved at a later time.)
All participants have now completed the leadership training and have considered whether or not they would like to lead a small group at this time. This was the original expectation of the training course, and it has now been honored.

F. To help people understand what is involved in starting a new group, present the material found in appendix I in lecture-discussion format. (Take 10-15 minutes.)

G. Take five minutes and briefly review the importance of building a supportive climate early in a group's life. Refer participants back to the "sharing questions" in appendix E. Point out that sharing of members' life stories or faith journeys is an especially useful way for a group to develop cohesion during the first several meetings. Because a supportive climate takes two to four weeks to develop, leaders should prepare enough "sharing questions" and/or other ways for members to get to know one another well.

Topic 3: Handling Difficulties within a Small Group

Strategies

A. Introduce the topic by leading a fifteen- to twenty-minute large-group discussion around participants' "homework" lists of difficulties. Though a group begins with clear agreements about its purpose, activities, and interaction, and though it builds a supportive climate, it can expect to experience periodic difficulties that require special attention by the group and its leader. Your participants can anticipate some of these difficulties and gain confidence that their groups will be able to handle the problems they encounter. Because many of these difficulties will be familiar to your participants, and because many require common-sense solutions, a general group discussion based on participants' "homework" lists will address most difficulties.

B. During the discussion, refer to the common group problems that Clyde Reid identifies in *Groups Alive—Church Alive*:

- Apathy
- The dominator
- Superficiality and frustration
- Avoidance of depth
- Unconscious group decisions
- Probing too deeply
- Self-centeredness
- Power cliques
- Inappropriate settings
- Failure to meet members' needs
- Relationships among members.

Reid's primary recommendation for dealing with most group difficulties is not surprising: face them directly and openly as a group. Reid comments: "In all these group problems, there is nothing like the openness and honest sharing of feelings as a general prescription for group health. This honesty has a price. It may be painful. But pain is often the necessary prelude to health."[13]

In my experience, Reid is right, even though the adage "easier said than done" frequently applies—especially to the problems of the dominator and superficiality. Unless groups face such major problems directly, however, they are apt to drift into mediocrity and eventually some members may quietly leave the group.

Emphasize that dominating and judgmental behaviors threaten a group's very existence. Such behaviors stifle other group members' freedom to participate and be themselves. Without a commitment to dialogue, a group simply cannot be a group.

Likewise, superficial group interaction is not fulfilling for most members and is also apt to destroy a group if members allow such behavior to continue.

C. During the discussion point out that a group can address such major problems directly during *regularly scheduled review sessions* if they are built into group life. If, of course, the dominating, judgmental, or superficial behavior is the result of a group member's deep-seated need for personal counseling or therapy, then the periodic review session can be a redemptive experience for this member. In particular, provide such a person feedback on specific behavior and encourage him or her to seek counseling.

D. In sum, help participants see that while groups are typically reluctant to face such difficulties directly and openly because they are understandably afraid of pain and conflict, leaders can help their groups put things in perspective by having the courage to: (1) face the pain and creatively manage the conflict or (2) face the likelihood that the group's very life may be on the line.

E. A group's reluctance to face the painful price of open and honest sharing of feelings is often related to an inability to *manage conflict*. Do not underestimate this problem, for few people know how to manage conflict effectively.

Time constraints do not permit use of role plays and other skill-building activities to develop competence in conflict management. (In fact, that requires a separate training course.) So take another ten to fifteen minutes in further general group discussion about managing conflict.

Point out that when facing conflict, the attitude group members take toward one another is especially important. For example, it is immensely helpful for group members to view one another as *different* rather than as *difficult*. As C. Jeff Woods states in *We've Never Done It Like This Before: 10 Creative Approaches to the Same Old Church Tasks*, "indisputably, people have different needs, take in information differently, make decisions according to different criteria, and see the world from different perspectives."[14] Fixing blame or judging someone as difficult seldom helps a group manage conflict. When faced with difficulties, what matters is how group members go about handling their differences.

F. Suggest principles for managing conflict such as:

• Program into our mental computers and use three sensible, simple questions to keep our differences clear and give direction to the conflict management process:

1. What are we differing about? (First clarify the primary issue.)
2. What do we each want? (Next clarify our goals.)
3. What other options do we have? (Fiinally seek creative, mutually agreeable alternatives.)

• Frequently check our perceptions; a high percentage of unproductive conflict comes from *misunderstanding*. (Clarifications: "So the way you see it is. . . . Have I understood you correctly?" Or, "Please paraphrase your understanding of my meaning.")

• Use I-messages or own your own judgments, because so much unproductive conflict comes from close-minded, judgmental attitudes. ("The way I see it is. . . . How do you see it?")

• Identify and express our feelings. ("Right now I feel . . . ")

• Take a problem-solving attitude rather than an adversarial approach. ("Let's explore our difference rather than prove who is right.")

• Work to diminish defensiveness and foster a supportive climate. (Remind participants of Jack Gibb's suggestions, from appendix D.)[15]

Recommend that participants recall and properly employ such principles when leading small groups. While the ability to manage conflict may minimize the pain of facing group difficulties, it will not eliminate a group's fear or experience of pain. I trust, however, that this session's discussion gives your participants confidence that they can help a group handle whatever difficulties it may face.

G. As closure for the training course and as a model of "ending" a group, use the final ten to fifteen minutes for celebration. Thank people for their participation and hard work. As a large group or in their small groups, ask people to talk about their concluding feelings (appreciations, hopes, fears). End with conversational prayer.

Conclusion

Our seven-week training course for potential small-group leaders is
complete. We now have newly trained small-group leaders some of
whom will soon be providing leadership for your congregation's small-
group ministry. Next we will consider the actual expansion process for
a church's small-group program. This process is our topic in the final
section, "The Expansion."

The Expansion

CHAPTER 7

Inaugurating New Small Groups

After your steering committee devotes ample attention to the twin components of planning and training, it should be ready to inaugurate new small groups. I find it helpful to think in terms of *phases* of group expansion as you will have an initial stage in which new groups get underway, followed by several additional stages of expansion in which more and more members of your congregation become involved in your small-group ministry.

If your church follows a quarterly church year, your first expansion phase will probably be three or four months long. (It could, however, continue throughout the year.) Because most churches normally have one or two start-up times during a year (September-October and January-February), it is important to schedule planning and training with a specific start-up date in mind.

For example, one church got off to an unnecessarily rocky start when it planned in the fall, trained in the winter, and began new groups in the spring, which was simply not a good start-up time in the church's life.

If your church hopes to inaugurate new groups in the fall, schedule planning a year in advance (the previous fall-winter) and training in the previous winter-spring. Winter expansion dates mean that you should schedule planning in the preceding winter-spring (or perhaps spring-summer) with training occurring during the fall. Remember that while your steering committee members may be available for planning during the summer, potential group leaders are typically unavailable for summertime training.

During the initial expansion period as many as one-third to one-half of your congregation may participate in your small-group ministry.[1]

During phase 2 (the second expansion period), from one-half to two-thirds of the congregation may well be participating. A leveling off period seems to occur in phase 3 (the third expansion phase). I trust, however, that most members of your congregation will participate over time in a small-group ministry where a sense of community is at the heart of the congregation's life and ministry.

Let's now consider each of these three phases of inaugurating new small groups.

Expansion Phase 1

Two topics warrant attention during the first phase of expansion: phase-1 interpretation and phase-1 implementation.

Phase-1 Interpretation

How will understanding and readiness for an expanded small-group ministry occur in your congregation? The answer to this question is no different from the presentation of other major programs in the life of the church. Your steering committee, then, can use the church's normal means of communication. For example, you can use the church newsletter and/or special mailings and your worship service to reach most of your congregational members.

A good goal for your steering committee's presentation task is to interpret the expanded small-group ministry so that all members of the congregation will choose whether or not to participate in a small group during the first expansion phase. Appropriate objectives to meet this goal include:

•   Developing a brochure that includes a statement of how small groups fit into your congregation's overall life and ministry, a statement of your small-group ministry's purpose and goals, a list of trained leaders, and descriptions of new, diverse small-group opportunities.

•   Placing your descriptive brochure in the hands of every member of your congregation.

*   Providing sign-up procedures and a description of the group forma-
    tion process.

An article or articles in the church's newsletter and/or special mailings can help augment these objectives. In fact, it is wise to write a
series of such articles to keep the congregation abreast of expansion
plans and progress. For example, write an article to explain the purpose,
goals, and strategy for the church's small-group ministry when your
church leaders adopt them. Then your steering committee can make
regular reports of its progress, including the recruiting and training of
potential leaders. Finally, once your steering committee knows which
new small groups it will add to existing small groups, prepare a brochure
or description sheet that features the church's complete small-group
opportunities; insert this in the newsletter and/or a special mailing.

Here is a sample of actual group descriptions from the brochure of
Northwood Presbyterian Church, Spokane, Washington:

FOCUS: Personal support. With opportunity to share those things in
our lives that matter most, this group will meet weekly to experience
care for one another in an atmosphere of informality and belonging,
openness and acceptance, helpfulness and supportiveness. Each group
member will have ample time to share personal concerns and to receive
support and prayer.

FOCUS: Coping with stress. This group will study the problem of
stress from a wide source of materials. We'll gain ideas on how to live
as Christians in an ever-changing world of increasing stress while draw-
ing upon each other for support in meeting these demands.

FOCUS: Peacemaking. This group will explore the issue of peacemaking as it relates to our Christian lives. Some of the questions we will
discuss are: How do we define peacemaking? Why should Christians be
involved in peacemaking? Is it a gospel imperative? Is the nuclear arms
arena just a political concern? What are other peacemaking and justice
issues where Christians can be involved?

FOCUS: Faith in action. The book of James superbly balances faith
and works. Through in-depth Bible study of this epistle, we hope to
grow into a group that will support each of us in thinking harder about
our faith, and living it out more fully each day.

FOCUS: Celebration of Discipline. This group is for those who wish to live deeper into their faith; for those who want to be closer to God; for those who dare to enter into the mysteries of the triune God. From reading and discussing Richard Foster's *Celebration of Discipline*, we will explore twelve classical spiritual disciplines. As Foster states, "The disciplines are meant to liberate us, not to bind us. They're meant to open us to the joy of the Lord."

FOCUS: Parents of young children. Parent(s), here's your chance to get out of the house and communicate with other adults, grow in your Christian faith, and receive support in raising a family. Babysitting will be available. Come, join us for a time of mental well-being and spiritual uplift.

FOCUS: Living the Adventure. This cassette tape series by Bruce Larson and Keith Miller offers opportunity for personal growth through study and sharing of our experiences with loneliness, rejection, possessions, change, and risk.

FOCUS: Breakfast group. This group will meet Wednesday mornings at 6:30 a.m. at a local restaurant. We'll have a devotional time and discussion guaranteed to wake you up!

FOCUS: Couple communication. We cannot not communicate! But at times we just don't do a very good job of it. This group is for partners who desire to deepen their communication skills so that they can enhance their already good relationship. The focus of the group experience will be in learning how to hear and respond more effectively.

FOCUS: 3-D Diet, Discipline, and Discipleship. Each weekly meeting includes weighing in, reciting memory verses, listening to taped teaching, sharing among group members, and praying together. If you desire to lose inches and grow in faith, then we're for you.

FOCUS: Pre-service prayer group. Come and pray during the thirty minutes preceding the Sunday morning worship service. We will share something from the scriptures and pray for our pastor, the choir, and the worship experience of the congregation as a whole. Prayer truly does change things—and people.

In worship services communicate similar information to what you present in your newsletter and/or special mailings. Bulletin announcements, minutes for mission, skits, and sermons are possible presentation means. Present occasional summaries of plans as they are adopted and implemented during the planning and training periods. Then provide weekly highlights during the month in which sign-ups occur.

Your pastor(s) can preach a sermon or a series of sermons to lend their support and provide sufficient biblical and theological bases for your church's expanding small-group ministry. One pastor, Rev. John B. Pierce, preached a six-week series on "The Church" during the inauguration of phase-1 expansion using the following sermon titles and texts:

- The People of God (Jer. 31:31-34; Titus 2:11-14; 3:3-7)
- The Body of Christ (Eph. 4:1-16; 1 Cor. 12:4-31)
- A Servant People (Mark 10:35-45; Rom. 12)
- Ministers of Reconciliation (2 Cor. 5:16-21)
- A Royal Priesthood (1 Pet. 2:1-10)
- Pastors, Ministers, and Ministry (Eph. 4:1-7, 11-16).

By using such presentation means as the church newsletter, a small-group ministry brochure, and worship services, all members of your congregation should know enough about phase-1 expansion plans and opportunities that they will be able to decide whether or not to participate in a small group.[2]

We are now ready to consider the implementation of phase-1 expansion.

Phase-1 Implementation

At the conclusion of your small-group leadership training course, the steering committee knows the number and type of new groups you will offer. Upon checking with the leaders of existing small groups and determining which groups will be ongoing, you will know the total number and type of small-group opportunities for phase-1 expansion.

As a check on congregational interest, prepare a simple questionnaire for people to complete in a worship service that asks them to check titles of groups that interest them and to request groups not on your list.

Questionnaire results can help the steering committee know the number and types of groups you'll need and identify interests you may overlook. Based on actual congregational interest and available group leadership, the steering committee may want to adjust the offerings for the first phase of small-group expansion.

Once the congregation knows which groups are available and members are ready to decide whether or not to participate in phase 1 of expansion, the steering committee should provide a way for people to sign up for the small-group opportunities. A useful procedure is to have people sign up for groups following a worship service during a fellowship or coffee hour. Display sign-up sheets for each group; include the group description and lines on which people can write their names; allow one line for each available opening. If some groups have limited openings, provide spaces for a waiting list. Allow enough room for members of the congregation to circulate and find the small group of their choice. Display your sign-up sheets on two consecutive Sundays to ensure that everyone has adequate opportunity to indicate interest.

Once everyone has a chance to sign up, the steering committee may need to assist group leaders in making decisions regarding group membership if some groups have too few or too many members. Groups can meet for the first time soon after the second week of sign-ups.

The steering committee should consult with group leaders to determine if group leaders want to meet together to finalize group membership decisions, to gain assistance in preparing for the first several group meetings, and to pray for one another.

Finally, the steering committee should set a time for group leaders to meet after their groups get underway, perhaps four to six weeks after groups begin. The purpose of such a meeting is to get a sense of how things are going and to determine what continuing support leaders feel they need, if any.

Typically, such a meeting is marked by excitement and anticipation, although several groups may be floundering and need suggestions for how to proceed. Occasionally, a group will simply not get off the ground and the leader will need assistance to determine how to get the group on a productive course or how to help the group terminate should this be the best course of action. The group leaders' meeting can conclude with prayer for one another and with a decision as to when, if at all, they would like to meet again.

In all likelihood, the next leaders' meeting will be at the end of the phase-1 expansion period at which time the steering committee can discern which groups will continue into phase 2 of expansion. In any event, the steering committee should keep in contact with group leaders during phase 1, to provide the support they'll need and to determine the planning and training necessary for future expansion.

Expansion Phase 2

During phase-1 implementation, the steering committee needs to plan the second phase of expansion. Three planning functions are especially important: (1) learning which groups will continue, which groups have space for new members, and which groups you should add to your small-group ministry; (2) presenting phase-2 opportunities to the congregation; and (3) scheduling training for new potential small-group leaders if you need new leaders for expansion phases 2 or 3. While enough trained leaders may be available for phase 2, you will no doubt need new leaders in phase 3.

From one-half to two-thirds of the congregation may well be participating in the small-group ministry during phase 2. In any event, most members of the congregation who desire to participate in a small group are probably now doing so. To involve the remainder of your congregation, the steering committee will need to become more active and creative in its interpretative tasks.

For example, when the steering committee identifies parishioners who are not participating in a small group, you might discover that some of these members already have quite a number of close personal relationships. On the other hand, the steering committee will probably identify a number of members who could greatly benefit from participating in a small group but who did not find the phase 1 or 2 timing suitable for their schedules. While some nonparticipants will probably involve themselves during phase 3 and beyond, other members may be hesitant. Personal contact with and invitation to these latter members may provide the necessary encouragement for them to sign up for future small groups.

Expansion Phase 3 and Beyond

At this point in the development of your church's small-group ministry, small groups will probably become "institutionalized." Your steering committee is likely to find itself making three primary contributions: program continuity, fresh resources, and new approaches.

First, you'll need to provide ongoing planning and training to continue offering attractive, diverse, well-led, and well-interpreted small groups for your congregation.

Second, some groups and their leaders may exhaust their resources for group life. This might be especially true of study groups. Your steering committee can help ongoing groups find fresh resources and ideas for continuing their life together.

And third, your steering committee should be aware that all good things tend to lose their value and spark without continual creative efforts. Your steering committee must work at discovering new, varied approaches, and not become complacent in what should be an exciting, dynamic adventure in your church's life and mission.

Conclusion

Small groups in the church can make your church come alive—this was the promise when we began. As your congregation develops its small-group ministry through proper attention to context, planning, training, and expansion, remember: Creating Christian community produces exactly the quality of life the majority of people on our planet desperately seek. I know for myself that there's nothing more important in my life than regularly participating in a sharing and support group—nothing!

Welcome to this incomparable, Life-giving ministry!

The Lord goes with us!

An Overview of Effective Small-Group Leadership

What makes small-group leaders effective? The question has been pursued by small-group researchers for years. Various answers have been advanced.

1930s and 1940s: Leadership Traits

It was first thought that all effective group leaders possess certain inherent *traits*. But no consensus of traits was forthcoming. It was not possible to separate the traits for effective and ineffective leaders.

1950s and 1960s: Leadership Style

In this period, theory of leadership effectiveness focused on leadership *style*. It was widely thought that effective leaders use a democratic leadership style while ineffective leaders use either a laissez faire or an authoritarian style. Again, research was unable to demonstrate that one leadership style was more effective than another. For example, some effective leaders use an authoritarian style while other effective leaders employ a democratic or a laissez faire style. On the other hand, some democratic leaders are ineffective, as are some authoritarian and laissez faire leaders.

1960s and 1970s: Contingency Model

Another approach to leadership effectiveness looks at leadership *style* but adds a new concept: the *situation* in which leadership occurs. Known as the "contingency model" of leadership effectiveness, this view suggests that leaders with a particular style are effective in some situations and ineffective in other situations. Specifically, this view deals with two particular leadership styles (relationship-oriented and task-oriented) and three factors of the leadership situation (structure, power, and leader-member relations).

Many studies found that relationship-oriented leaders are effective when the situational factors (structure, power, and leader-member relations) are moderately favorable to the leader. Task-oriented leaders, on the other hand, were consistently found to be effective when the situational factors were either strongly favorable or strongly unfavorable to the leader.

Theorists who advocate this view suggest that effective group leadership is contingent upon matching a person's leadership style with the situation in which that person is leading. This view of group leadership revolutionized the leadership world with its recommendation that situations, not people, need changing. The need, therefore, is to determine one's leadership style and then to engineer the situation to fit that style. For example, if I find that I have a relationship-oriented style, then I engineer the amount of group structure, the level of leader power, and the degree of leader-member relations to be moderately favorable to myself.

While the contingency view has strong proponents among small-group researchers and theorists, it is not without its detractors. Critics cite problems with the validity of the research upon which this view is based; they also question the way the approach is conceptualized. I find that the contingency view has some limitations, especially for leaders in volunteer organizations.

One limitation is conceptual and concerns the either-or nature of leadership style. Why cannot we have both a relationship-oriented and a task-oriented leadership style? I recommend a "combination" leadership style.

A second limitation of the contingency model is its application to volunteer leaders. Most contingency model research was conducted in profit-making, governmental, and business settings. While business and governmental leaders typically have much control over situational factors, that is not the case in many nonprofit, volunteer settings. In the volunteer sector, if a group member does not like the high level of structure or power with which a task-oriented leader proceeds, the member can simply challenge the situational framework and comfortably curtail participation. Because participation constraints are very different in volunteer and nonvolunteer settings, it may not always be possible to engineer the situation to be favorable to the leader. Leaders of volunteers may have to become flexible in their leadership style, adapting their style to situational exigencies whenever it is unacceptable to adapt the situation to their style.

1980s and Beyond: Flexible Theory

In response to possible limitations of the contingency approach to leadership effectiveness, a new view was introduced in the 1980s. This view is the *flexible or adaptable* theory of leadership. Here, it is leadership *behavior* that matters; that is, leaders should employ whatever leadership behaviors promote accomplishment of group purpose. When the situation calls for relationship-type leadership behaviors, a relationship-oriented style should be employed. On the other hand, when task-type behaviors are needed, leaders must be flexible enough to adapt their style and employ task-oriented behaviors.

To be effectively flexible prospective leaders need (1) adequate leadership style assessment procedures and (2) specification of effective and ineffective leadership characteristics. (See appendices B and C.)

The Value of the Flexible Approach in Church Groups

Because it is unrealistic, even unacceptable, in a church setting for the typical small-group leader to control or manage the level of group structure, leader power, and leader-member relations so that it is favorable to the leader's own style, I advise the adoption of this most recent, flexible or adaptable view of leadership. Let us more carefully examine the adaptable perspective.[1]

The adaptable approach to leadership effectiveness focuses on being flexible in one's leadership style to meet situational exigencies. If the situation is one that presents high or low levels of group structure, leader power, and leader-member relations, then an effectively trained leader can turn to a task-oriented style. Likewise, if the situation presents moderate levels of structure, power, and leader-member relations, an effectively trained leader can employ a relationship-oriented style. Finally, when situational factors change (to be more or less favorable to a leader), the leader can adapt to a more task- or relationship-orientation as appropriate.2

Before moving on to an application of this flexible view of leadership effectiveness, two important assumptions must be succinctly stated and kept in mind. First, our leaders should be able to employ both the relationship- and task-oriented styles of leadership. Second, it is possible to identify both effective and ineffective leadership behaviors. This means that (1) prospective leaders who have a predominantly task- or relationship-oriented style should work at developing both styles, and (2) prospective leaders should learn to employ specific effective leadership behaviors and avoid specific ineffective behaviors.

Leadership Style Inventory[1]

Instructions: The following six items describe various leadership characteristics. In responding, please describe the way *you typically act* when you lead a *small-group discussion.* Circle the number that best represents your leadership behavior, using a scale ranging from one (1) to six (6) with one (1) being "Never" or "Not At All" and six (6) being "Always" or "Completely." Work rapidly; your first answer is likely to be the most accurate.

When I lead a small-group discussion, I usually:

		Never, Not At All					Always, Completely
1.	Coordinate the work of others.	1	2	3	4	5	6
2.	Value the participation of others.	1	2	3	4	5	6
3.	Make sure that work is completed on time.	1	2	3	4	5	6
4.	Am sensitive to group mood.	1	2	3	4	5	6
5.	Offer procedural guidelines.	1	2	3	4	5	6
6.	Make others feel accepted and comfortable.	1	2	3	4	5	6

Scoring for the Leadership Style Inventory is fairly simple.

Look at items 1, 3, and 5. How many times did you circle the number 5 or 6? Write that number here:
____ This number (0-3) is your task-oriented score.

Look at items 2, 4, and 6. How many times did you circle the number 5 or 6? Write that number here:
___ This number (0-3) is your relationship-oriented score.

To interpret your style orientation, use the following scoring grid:

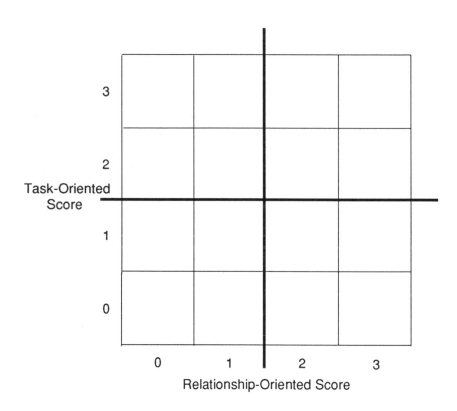

Plot your score onto the grid. For example, if your task-oriented score is 0 (zero) and your relationship-oriented score is 3, put an X in the "box" at the bottom far right corner of the grid. If your task-oriented score is 3 and your relationship-oriented score is 2, put an X in the "box" that is in the top line, second from the right.

Determine which quadrant your score puts you in:

If your scores fit into the lower right quadrant, you have a *relationship-oriented* leadership style.

If your scores fit into the upper left quadrant, you have a *task-oriented* leadership style.

If your scores fit into the lower left quadrant, you have an *undeveloped* leadership style.

If your scores fit into the upper right quadrant, you have a *combination* leadership style (combination of highly rated task- and relationship-oriented items).

There are several important advantages of using the Leadership Style Inventory, including:

• It is quick and easy to administer and interpret.
• It has a proven record of high validity.
• It is able to overcome the *either* task- *or* relationship-style limitation of the contingency model because it allows for the undeveloped- and combination-style orientations, which include *both* task *and* relationship behaviors.
• It can reveal a person's need or potential for style development. For example, if you have an undeveloped leadership style, your potential for task- and relationship-oriented behaviors is not yet expressed; if you have a relationship style, you can still develop your task-oriented behavior.

As I point out in appendix A regarding effective small-group leadership, the ability to be flexible and to adapt leadership behavior to situational demands is especially important for small-group leaders in voluntary organizations such as the church. Because leaders must have both task- and relationship-oriented skills if they are to be flexible in their leadership behavior, the combination leadership style is preferable for church small-group leaders.

This means that undeveloped, task-oriented, and relationship-oriented leaders can be encouraged to expand their leadership potential by developing competency in complementary behaviors. While combination leaders already have the ability to employ both task- and relationship-oriented behaviors, these leaders can be encouraged to make their strengths even stronger by expanding their competencies.

Characteristics of Effective and Ineffective Small-Group Discussion Leaders

To assist leaders in identifying specific leadership behaviors to develop or avoid, here is a list of characteristics for effective and ineffective small-group discussion leaders.[1]

Characteristics of Effective Small-Group Discussion Leaders

1. Shows and Fosters Friendliness

A. Relational Qualities

- Is open, not judgmental
- Is egalitarian
- Is sensitive to all group members
- Shows warmth
- Is confident
- Is outgoing
- Is positive
- Displays love

B. Group Atmosphere

- Makes members feel comfortable and at ease
- Creates a sharing environment
- Builds a trust level

- Helps members feel free to contribute
- Encourages open, friendly discussion
- Fosters a pleasant atmosphere

C. *Responsive Listening*

- Honors and accepts all contributions
- Treats all members with respect
- Makes all members feel valued
- Listens actively to all members
- Respects all opinions
- Shows appreciation and support of members

D. *Encourages Sharing*

- Allows God to bring group together
- Encourages shy members to participate
- Helps members get acquainted
- Fosters cooperation
- Allows objections to surface

2. Provides Orientation: Gives Task Direction

A. *As the Meeting Starts*

- Enables group to get started
- Provides an agenda
- Knows material to be discussed
- Prepares and asks questions to facilitate interaction
- Clearly introduces and explains topic
- Describes group goal

B. *As the Meeting Continues*

- Coordinates task
- Keeps group moving
- Keeps situation under control

- Guides discussion without forcing it
- Keeps group on topic
- Keeps group focused on questions
- Holds group to agenda
- Redirects group as needed
- Attempts to deal with all agenda items
- Gauges time
- Helps eliminate tangents

C. As the Meeting Finishes

- Ends topics when contributions cease
- Accomplishes goal of discussion

3.   Provides Orientation: Gives Procedural Direction

A. Clarifies Expectations

- Briefs group on task and on time available
- Lets members know what is expected of them
- Has an outline

B. Comments about Group Process

- Points out important things members say
- Provides clarification of comments and process
- Summarizes any consensus
- Sums up discussion to everyone's satisfaction

4.   Asks for Information and Opinions

A. Facilitates Participation

- Makes sure everyone has opportunity to participate
- Meaningfully involves everyone in discussion
- Develops responses from the group

B. Facilitates Interaction

- Helps members respond to one another's contributions
- Helps quiet members express thoughts
- Keeps members from dominating the discussion

C. Facilitates Understanding

- Fosters understanding and clarity of members' viewpoints
- Picks up on high points to allow further comment by others
- Helps participants expand on ideas

Characteristics of Ineffective Small-Group Discussion Leaders

1. Shows Antagonism

A. In Position

- Sets self as authority
- Claims status differential
- Uses leader position to monopolize discussion
- Controls the discussion
- Is opinionated; biased
- Gives own opinions as fact
- Is too rigid in protocol and agenda

B. In Attitude

- Makes people feel uncomfortable
- Expresses threatening attitude
- Does not listen
- Does not value members' opinions
- Is defensive toward what is said
- Is insensitive to what members say or want to say
- Disregards members' contributions
- Judges members' comments; condemns

C. In Interaction

- Puts people down
- Dominates discussion
- Fails to recognize or be receptive to contributions from others
- Puts people off
- Interrupts or stifles creativity of thought

2.   Shows Tension

- Does not allow open exchange of information and opinions
- Needs resolution of all disagreements
- Puts people on the spot
- Is apologetic
- Fears silence
- Is insecure; not confident

3.   Shows Disagreeableness

- Contradicts
- Takes sides on issues
- Is mute on some points while agreeing on others
- Ignores members with different opinions

4.   Gives Little Orientation

A. As the Meeting Starts

- Is not clear on purpose
- Is uncertain about what is required
- Fails to provide group direction
- Does not define issues
- Has poorly thought out discussion questions
- Does not make sure issues and questions are understood
- Provides too narrow focus

B. As the Meeting Continues

- Does not keep discussion moving
- Does not keep group on issue; loses focus
- Allows discussion to become irrelevant or unrelated to topic
- Lets discussion wander or digress
- Lets group flounder
- Lets members dominate discussion
- Does not keep track of time limits
- Tries to go too fast
- Stays on one topic too long
- Loses track of topic
- Lets discussion become too personal

C. As the Meeting Finishes

- Does not summarize discussion
- Does not bring discussion to a conclusion

5. Asks for Little Information and Opinions

- Does not invite member responses
- Fails to allow members to express themselves fully
- Encourages talkative members
- Overlooks quiet members

6. Gives Too Much Information and Too Many Opinions

- Talks too much
- Expresses too much personal opinion
- Makes irrelevant comments
- Does not stay on subject; wanders or rambles
- Answers own questions

Certain categories in these lists refer to relationship-oriented behaviors: Shows and Fosters Friendliness; Shows Antagonism; Shows Tension; and Shows Disagreeableness.

These categories refer to task-oriented behaviors: Provides Orientation; Asks for Information and Opinions; Gives Little Orientation; Asks for Little Information and Opinions; and Gives Too Much Information and Too Many Opinions.

Developing a Supportive Group Climate

To have a supportive group climate in which members feel free to be themselves, we need to create an atmosphere of openness and acceptance.

Attitudes and Behaviors

Several attitudes or behaviors help a supportive climate develop in a group. An "interest in one another's interests" can provide a basis for trust and vitality to emerge in a group's life. Such genuine, active interest can help members know they are taken seriously, and it can lead to support for working through members' life concerns. Also, members can feel a tremendous "liberation" when they sense a growing freedom to be themselves; when it becomes okay to say what they want, in the way they want; when they experience a nonjudgmental attitude from the others.

Small-group research suggests that certain attitudes and behaviors usually precipitate supportiveness in a group while other qualities lead to defensiveness. Specifically, group researcher and consultant Jack Gibb consistently found that feelings of personal threat or defensiveness diminish when relationships among group members are characterized by:

- description rather than evaluation
- problem orientation rather than control
- spontaneity rather than strategy
- empathy rather than neutrality
- equality rather than superiority
- provisionalism rather than certainty.[1]

My own empirical research suggests that the most satisfying supportive relationships develop where group members experience:

- openness
- acceptance
- warmth
- personal growth.[2]

Agreements and "Sharing Questions"

Finally, there are two very practical matters that all groups should consider when they desire to build a supportive climate among group members: establishment of agreements about group life and use of "sharing questions."

Because both of these practical matters deserve our closer attention, let's consider each in some detail. Here we'll examine the matter of creating agreements about group life. Appendix E lists possible "sharing questions."

Small-group research consistently reveals that the two most important variables in group leadership are clarity of group purpose and clarity of member participation.[3] Members need to know where their group is going and how they may contribute to group interaction.

They can gain this desirable clarity if the group establishes some initial agreements about their group's purpose and interaction. Without such agreements, many groups operate without focus and quickly experience dynamics that stifle group interaction.

To develop consensus about group purpose and interaction, each member can formulate and propose a statement of the group's purpose and the members' participation. The leader may be especially helpful in suggesting possible options, but care must be taken not to stifle member creativity and not to make decisions for the group.

We'll consider important elements of such statements of agreement in detail in unit 5, under the topic "Forming New Groups." (See appendix I.)

Likewise, in unit 2 we'll examine suggestions for group members that can enhance member participation. (See appendix F.)

"Sharing Questions" for Building a Supportive Group Climate

The use of "sharing questions" for building a supportive climate is particularly valuable early in a group's life. Sharing questions can be a natural medium to help group members get acquainted with one another. They are particularly useful during the first two or three meetings or until such time as the group feels like "a group." When such cohesion exists, group members usually feel comfortable and free to be open with one another. Here are two dozen suggested questions that can be useful in building a supportive climate in a group. Questions 1 and 24 are particularly useful when members are getting acquainted with one another.

Twenty-Four Questions to Facilitate Getting Acquainted

1. What are one or two of the most important things that have happened in your life during the last week?

2. What are three or four words that best describe you?

3. What is one of the best things that has happened to you in the last several years?

4. If you were to draw a coat of arms for yourself, what symbol would you put on it?

5. What is something you feel a little unsure of about yourself?

6. What are one or two major changes you have made in your life?

7. What are two or three of your most meaningful achievements?

8. Describe one of your happiest memories and/or most significant events.

9. What are two or three things you like about yourself?

10. What are two or three things you do very well? How about a day-to-day hang-up?

11. If you could change several things about your life right now, what might they be?

12. In what do you most trust?

13. Who are two people in the world you would most like to meet?

14. If you won $50,000, how would you spend it?

15. Who is the most authentic person you have ever met?

16. Who or what is someone/something you admire/don't admire?

17. What would you most like to do or be in the next five years if there were no limitations and you knew you would not fail?

18. What or where is a happy place for you?

19. Complete the sentence: "It would give me real happiness to . . . "

20. What is a present you would most like to receive?

21. What do you do for fun or in your free time?

22. What is one of your pet peeves?

23. What is your favorite animal, color, T.V. program, music, or . . .?

24.   What are two or three of the most significant influences (persons, events, places) that have helped shape your life?

Trainer: Questions 1 and 24 are good questions to use in the leadership training course to help participants get acquainted. When used in training with groups of three to five, they can function as a model for building a supportive climate.

Seven Spiritual "Sharing Questions"

Questions of a distinctly spiritual nature such as the following can also help build a supportive climate in a group:

1.   When did you first begin to realize that God loves you, if ever?

2.   When, if ever, did God become more than a word for you? When, if ever, did God become a living Being for you?

3.   What are your strongest convictions about God?

4.   If you could hear God say one thing to you, what do you think God would say? If you could say one thing to God, what would you say?

5.   What single question do you most want God to answer for you?

6.   Describe the person you have known who you felt knew God most intimately?

7.   How would you describe your "life-story" or "faith journey"?

Note regarding question 7: This question requires further comment. While it is possible to treat it as any other question, it is also possible to build a great deal of the getting-acquainted period around this question. In fact, it is possible to spend two or three meetings early in the group's life on this question. Frequently it takes group members twenty to forty minutes each to respond fully. If a group uses this question in this manner, it is likely to "become a group" following completion of the question.

Here is a way to use this question to build such a supportive climate in a group:

1.   Have group members reflect on the major stages of their lives (childhood, teenage years, young adulthood) and identify the main events, people, and places that have deeply influenced them both positively and negatively in each period.

2.   Have each person draw a time-line of the main influences for each period and/or divide a paper into sections, one per stage, and draw something that represents the main influences for each period. (Use a representative color, if possible.) Also include a summary phrase that best describes each period.

3.   Take time for each member adequately to share her of his life story/ faith journey, usually twenty to forty minutes per person. An alternate way to conduct the session is for each member to relate only one life-stage at a time.

Suggestions for Facilitating Member Participation

Potter and Andersen present the following sixteen suggestions in their most helpful chapter on the rarely treated topic of "Improving Participation in Discussion":

1. **Listen critically and thoughtfully to others.** Seek the other person's point of view; probe for new information and opinion. But don't accept unsupported generalizations. *Remember: Use your critical faculties when listening.*

2. **Be sure you know the goal of the discussion at the start.** Don't let the discussion get too far along without knowing the goal or goals of the group. Ask for definitions of terms, basic issues of the topic, and important background material. *Remember: If you do not know where you are going, you may never get there.*

3. **Speak your mind freely.** Discussion is based on the exchange of ideas. No one else has your specific background of knowledge and experience. You help by sharing your ideas. *Remember: You have a responsibility besides that of listening.*

4. **Strike while the iron is hot.** Don't wait to speak until you are called on. You may forget your point or miss the best time to present it. *Remember: If you wait too long, the point may be lost.*

5. **Let the other person talk, too.** Don't speak for more than a minute or two at a time. Make your point in as few words as possible. *Remember: It makes little difference who carries the ball as long as it's carried.*

6. **Don't let the discussion get away from you.** If you do not understand, say so tactfully. Ask questions until you do understand. Other members of the group may also feel that a point is unclear and be grateful for your initiative. *Remember: You cannot make wise decisions later if they are based on misunderstanding.*

7. **Don't fight over the ownership of ideas.** Once you have given an idea to the group, let it become the group's property. Don't feel that you must defend it just because it was yours. *Remember: The aim of the discussion is to explore ideas, not to win your point.*

8. **Indulge in friendly disagreement.** When you disagree with a point that is made, say so, and tell why. But do it in a friendly way. It is not necessary to "clobber" the individual and her or his ideas. *Remember: Raw emotion can hinder sound thinking.*

9. **Stay on the beam.** Because digressions usually hinder progress, keep your remarks relevant. Show how your points are related to the discussion. Don't repeat what has already been covered. *Remember: You should not ride personal hobbyhorses in discussion.*

10. **Try to maintain an open mind.** Discussion is not debate. You do not have to commit yourself irrevocably to a case or idea. Seek facts and the factual basis for opinions. Try to be unprejudiced and objective. *Remember: The other side is also based upon facts and logic.*

11. **Come to the discussion prepared to participate.** Before the discussion, think through the issues involved in a topic. Consider what facts may be needed. Study the topic. Make a list of questions you would like to have answered. *Remember: Advance preparation is a necessary condition for successful discussion.*

12. **Try to make the discussion a pleasant experience for all.** Don't take yourself too seriously in discussion. Try to get some fun out of it and make it pleasant for others, too. A laugh or pointed joke can dispel glumness, hostility, and boredom. *Remember: A smile may do more to further the discussion than your best argument.*

13. **Help others to participate.** There may be some in the group who would like to participate but are too timid. Help the leader draw them out. Their knowledge and opinions are important. Call them by name, refer questions to them, or point out the need for hearing from everyone. *Remember: The resources in a discussion group cannot be used unless they are tapped.*

14. **Chart the progress of the discussion.** Ask for occasional summaries or give them yourself. Call attention to the group's goals and the progress made toward those goals. Point out the ground yet to be covered. *Remember: The capable mariner frequently checks to see where she or he is.*

15. **Avoid interrupting the progress of the discussion.** Try to do only those things that expedite—not block—the discussion. Avoid loud and lengthy side conversations with your neighbors, withdrawing from the discussion, excessive reaction, dogmatic statements, or annoying physical activities. *Remember: Be a booster, not a blocker.*

16. **Keep the communication channels open.** Be sure you listen to what is being said. Don't direct your remarks only to the leader or a few members; include the entire group. Try to make your language clear and temperate. Check to see that you have been understood. Ask others to clarify unclear points. *Remember: In discussion you should beam the message so that your meaning is interpreted as you mean it to be.*

(This list is excerpted with slight amendment from David Potter and Martin Andersen, *Discussion: A Guide to Effective Practice*, 1st ed. [Belmont, Calif.: Wadsworth, 1963], 36-38. Used by permission.)

The Inductive Method of Group Discussion

The key to most effective group study is well framed and properly used discussion questions. Questions thrust group members into the study material, stimulate group interaction that processes the material, and enable members to make the material relevant to the group and members' lives.

While some groups may use a study guide that supplies discussion questions, group leaders must be able to evaluate and adapt questions for their groups' needs. Then many times no adequate discussion guide is available and leaders must create effective discussion questions by themselves. How, then, can prospective group leaders learn to formulate and use discussion questions that foster effective group inquiry?

The inductive method is one of the best inquiry methods to learn; it can foster serious, stimulating, and relevant discussion of study material. This method does not depend on outside experts or members' preconceived notions about a subject; it uses the group's own resources and attempts to let the material speak for itself.

The inductive method moves from observation to interpretation to application. It asks,

- What does the material *say*? (Observation or knowledge questions.)

- What does it *mean*? (Interpretation or understanding questions.)

- What does it *mean to us*? (Application or evaluation questions.)

To study adequately a particular passage of material, it is usually necessary to prepare two or three questions for each level of inquiry. (A "passage" may be from the Bible or from some other source.)

Example: The following is a passage from Robert Leslie's book *Sharing Groups in the Church.* After the passage I give sample discussion questions at each level (observation, interpretation, application). As trainer you can use these questions to lead a group study of the Leslie passage.

Book Excerpt

Most plans for Bible study begin with a scholarly approach to the story being discussed with reference to commentaries, research studies, accounts of life in Palestine in the first century, and the like. I think that most people lose interest in Bible study because of this very approach. The implication is that the scholar is the one who is best equipped to make use of the Bible. I recognize the need for biblical scholarship, but I think it tends to be brought in prematurely. If people are led to believe that they must become experts in biblical history and interpretation in order to use the Bible, their interest diminishes at the onset. I prefer to present the Bible as a document of timeless experiences which everyone knows something about.

(From Robert Leslie, *Sharing Groups in the Church* [Nashville: Abingdon, 1971], 35.)

Discussion Questions

Observation-Knowledge Questions: "What does it say?"

1. What does Leslie think happens in most studies?
2. What does Leslie think should happen in studies?

Interpretation-Understanding Questions: "What does it mean?"

1.   What does Leslie mean by a scholarly approach?
2.   Why does Leslie prefer that participants be the experts?

Application-Evaluation Questions: "What does it mean to us?"

1.   Why does a concern about how we approach study make a differ
     ence?
2.   What has been your experience with scholarly and/or personal
     studies? Which do you prefer and why?

Selected Study Resources

Inductive Study

* *Equip* by Lindell Sawyers (Geneva Press, 1972).
* *Leading Bible Discussions* by James Nyquist and Jack Kuhatschek (InterVarsity Press, 1985).

Relational Study

* Various *Serendipity* Bible studies available from Serendipity Small Group Resources (Littleton, Colo.).

* *Transforming Bible Study* by Walter Wink (Abingdon, 1989).

Social Action

* *Keeping and Healing the Creation* (Committee on Social Witness Policy, Presbyterian Church USA, 1989).

* *Taking Charge: Personal and Political Change through Simple Living* by the Simple Living Collective, American Friends Service Committee (Bantam, 1977).

* *Ideas for Social Action* by Anthony Campolo (Zondervan, 1983).

Christian Formation

- *A Tree Full of Angels* by Macrina Wiederkehr (HarperCollins, 1990).

- *Accountable Discipleship* by David Watson (Discipleship Resources, 1984).

- *Celebration of Discipline* by Richard Foster (Harper & Row, 1978).

- *Reformed Spirituality* by Howard Rice (Westminster, 1992).

Personal Growth

- *A Hunger for Healing*, a videotape series by J. Keith Miller (Harper & Row, 1992).

- *Caring Enough to Be Heard* by David Augsburger (Regal, 1982).

- *Growth Groups* by Howard Clinebell (Abingdon, 1977).

- *The Different Drum* by M. Scott Peck (Simon & Schuster, 1987).

Starting New Groups

Clarifying Purpose and Activities

During a group's first several meetings, the leader can be especially help-ful as the group establishes its purpose, its agreements about group life, and a supportive group climate.

A description of the group (as printed in a brochure or church news-letter, for instance) may have expressed the group's purpose, but mem-bers need to discuss their expectations for the group and arrive at a con-sensus about the group's reason for existence. The printed group de-scription may also have listed group activities, but *the group* needs to decide which activities will be primary and secondary in its life. Without agreement about group purpose and activities, members may soon pull against one another and experience stress and frustration that prevent the group from being effective.

If it becomes apparent that the group cannot accommodate all the central desires of its members, the group should decide which purpose and activities it will have so that members not sharing these interests can find another group.

Making Agreements about Group Life

Once a group clarifies and adopts its purpose and activities, the group itself should decide in general terms how it will operate.[1] Agreements about *meeting frequency, length, place,* and *duration* are usually easy to make once the group decides on its purpose and activities.

For example, a sharing group will no doubt want to meet weekly for several hours in members' homes. To clarify expectations, it is good to agree on a date when the group will disband or "regroup" and make new decisions about its future. Such agreement gives members who may decide to leave the group a natural, smooth way to depart. Normally groups will follow the same pattern used for Sunday school classes. Phase 1 of group expansion, covered in chapter 7, usually lasts three to four months. This means that most groups operate on an annual basis, with opportunity provided to continue, leave, or join the group halfway through the year. In any event, your steering committee will need to coordinate carefully the scheduling of group offerings.

Some additional agreements about group life to consider include *group size* and *inclusion of new members*. Again, the group's purpose and activities will greatly help determine such agreements. For example, it is difficult for a sharing group that meets weekly for several hours to accommodate more than six to eight members or frequently to go through the cohesion process necessitated by the addition of new members.

From the beginning, times of *regular review* (once every two to four months) should also be built into the group life so that groups can keep on course and prevent minor difficulties from growing into major problems.

Finally, it helps to have a few agreements about *group interaction,* including clarity about participation and attendance. For example, the group may decide that (1) that attendance is expected except for unforeseen circumstances and (2) while group members should feel free to participate equally in group interaction, it is always all right to "pass" without explanation in group discussion. The group must also clarify its agreements about *confidentiality.*

For additional suggestions concerning a small-group agreement or contract, see Arthur R. Baranowski, *Creating Small Faith Communities* (St. Anthony Messenger, 1988), 101.

Introduction

1. Robert Wuthnow, *Sharing the Journey: Support Groups and America's New Quest for Community* (New York: Free Press, 1994).

Chapter 1

1. I use *Life,* with a capital L, to refer to our present experience of Life in the kingdom of God, of Life in the body of Christ; it is our Life together through Christian community.

2. See Gerhard Kittel, ed., *Theological Dictionary of the New Testament,* trans. Geoffrey W. Bromiley, vol. 3 (Grand Rapids: Eerdmans, 1965), 797, for an exposition of this point. For a discussion of the Septuagint's rendering of the Hebrew *chabar* (or more commonly *havurot*) as *koinonia,* see G. Johannes Botterweck and Helmer Ringgren, eds., *Theological Dictionary of the Old Testament,* trans. David E. Green, vol. 4 (Grand Rapids: Eerdmans, 1980), 197; and Alan Richardson, ed., *A Theological Word Book of the Bible* (New York: Macmillan, 1962), 81.

3. M. Scott Peck, *The Different Drum: Community-Making and Peace* (New York: Simon & Schuster, 1987), 27-28.

4. Ibid., 57, 59.

5. Ibid., 68.

6. Ibid., 77-78.

7. Ibid., 84.

8. John Claypool, *The Preaching Event* (Waco, Tex.: Word, 1980), 73-75.

9. Charles Gerkin, *Prophetic Pastoral Practice: A Christian Vision of Life Together* (Nashville: Abingdon, 1991).

10. Evelyn Eaton Whitehead and James D. Whitehead, *Community of Faith: Models and Strategies for Developing Christian Communities* (New York: Seabury, 1982).

11. Seymour B. Sarason, *The Psychological Sense of Community: Prospects for a Community Psychology* (San Francisco: Jossey-Bass, 1974).

12. Paul Hanson, *The People Called: The Growth of Community in the Bible* (San Francisco: Harper & Row, 1987), 501.

13. See Parker J. Palmer, "A Place Called Community," *Christian Century,* 16 March 1977.

14. See Robert Kysar, *Called to Care: Biblical Images for Social Ministry* (Minneapolis: Fortress, 1991).

15. Hanson, *The People Called,* 501.

16. Robert Leslie, *Sharing Groups in the Church* (Nashville: Abingdon, 1971), 63.

17. See Dietrich Bonhoeffer, *The Communion of Saints: A Dogmatic Inquiry into the Sociology of the Church,* trans. R. Gregor Smith (New York: Harper & Row, 1963).

18. Hanson, *The People Called,* 501.

19. See Leslie, *Sharing Groups in the Church,* 120-21. Palmer also makes this point in "A Place Called Community," 255. See also Paul Tournier, *Escape from Loneliness,* trans. John S. Gilmour (Philadelphia: Westminster, 1962).

20. Leslie, *Sharing Groups in the Church,* 121-22. Also see Palmer, "A Place Called Community," 253.

21. Leslie, *Sharing Groups in the Church,* 185.

22. James H. Forest, *Making Friends of Enemies: Reflections on the Teachings of Jesus* (New York: Crossroad, 1987), 44-46.

23. I develop this point more fully in chapter 2.

24. See Thomas Kirkpatrick, "Conceptualizing and Developing Community in a Congregation" (D. Min. diss., San Francisco Theological Seminary, 1978).

Chapter 2

1. Patrick J. Brennan, aware of similar models in the Third World (notably Latin American base communities and Korean home cell groups), challenges Catholic churches to re-imagine the parish as a "community of communities"; see *Re-Imagining the Parish: Base Communities,*

Adulthood, and Family Consciousness (New York: Crossroad, 1990), 56-57. Arthur R. Baranawski presents specific plans for developing Catholic parish life and mission around small groups; see *Creating Faith Communities: A Plan for Restructuring the Parish and Renewing Catholic Life* (Cincinnati: St. Anthony Messenger, 1988).

2. A parallel development of community exists among Jews through the Havurot movement. In fact, attempts to organize Jews to study, socialize, and celebrate in small, face-to-face havurot groups are known to have existed more than two thousand years ago; see "Valley Beth Shalom Havurah Packet," *Raayonot* 3, no. 3 (Summer 1983): 25-26. But it was not until the 1970s, that the notion of havurot began to impact synagogue life. Through havurot programs, both traditional Jews and the Jewish counterculture are experiencing a revival of Jewish life and practice, an avenue to develop friendship and fellowship, and a medium to attract and integrate new members into temple life. A leading havurot expert, Rabbi Harold Schulwcis, cites openness, personal involvement, belonging, patience, and balance among study, socializing, social action, and prayer as essential characteristics of havurot; see "A Statement on the Havurah," *Raayonot* 3, no. 3 (Summer 1983): 29-32. Just as we found with koinonia in Christian churches, so also the meaning and intimacy experienced in havurot can revitalize, even restructure, synagogues.

Significantly, the Havurot movement has broad participation among American Judaism. In fact, Riv-Ellen Prell points out that many American Jews from Conservative, Reform, and Reconstructionist synagogues prefer small havurot groups to large, impersonal synagogue gatherings; see *Prayer and Community: The Havurah in American Judaism* (Detroit: Wayne State University, 1989), 16. William Novak also finds the influences of the major denominations on havurot very apparent; see "From Somerville to Savannah. . .and Los Angeles. . . and Dayton. . .," *Moment* 6, no. 2 (January-February 1981): 59. The common denominator of every havurot, however, is its small size and quality of intimacy and sharing.

For additional reading on the Havurot movement, see: Moshe Halfon, "Havurot Then and Now: The Reconstructionist Connection," *Raayonot* 3, no. 3 (Summer 1983): 4-13; The National Havurah Conference, "Havurah," *Sh'ma*, 7 September 1979, 121-131; Jacob Neusner, ed., *Contemporary Judaic Fellowship in Theory and in Practice* (New

York: Ktav, 1972); Michael Strassfeld, "Havurot," *Present Tense* 8, no.
3 (Spring 1980): 29-31; Arthur Waskow, *These Holy Sparks: The Rebirth of the Jewish People* (San Francisco: Harper & Row, 1983); Harry
Wasserman, Gerald B. Bubis, and Alan Lert, "The Concept of Havurah:
An Analysis," *Journal of Reform Judaism* 26 (Winter 1979), 35-50.

3. Lyle E. Schaller, "Looking at the Small Church: A Frame of
Reference," *Christian Ministry* 8, no. 4 (1977): 5-9.

4. Ibid., 7. For an elaboration of this point, see Paul Fromer,
"Earth Movers and Fog Clouds," *His* 29, no. 2 (November 1968): 9-13.

5. Robert Leslie, *Sharing Groups in the Church* (Nashville:
Abingdon, 1971), 14.

6. Roy M. Oswald, *How to Build a Support System for Your Ministry* (Washington, D.C.: The Alban Institute, 1991), 96.

7. Howard J. Clinebell, Jr., *The People Dynamic: Changing Self
and Society through Growth Groups* (New York: Harper & Row, 1972),
vii. Other contemporary authors also point to the importance of small
groups in developing a sense of community in our churches: Leonardo
Boff, *Ecclesiogenesis: The Base Communities Reinvent the Church*
(Maryknoll, N.Y.: Orbis, 1986); Kennon L. Callahan, *Twelve Keys to
an Effective Church: Strategic Planning for Mission* (San Francisco:
Harper & Row, 1983); Roy M. Oswald, *Finding Balance for Effective
Ministry* (Washington, D.C.: The Alban Institute, 1991); Lyle E.
Schaller, *Assimilating New Members* (Nashville: Abindgon, 1978); Lyle
E. Schaller, *Choices for Churches* (Nashville: Abingdon, 1990); Donald
P. Smith, *Congregations Alive* (Philadelphia: Westminster, 1981);
Robert Wuthnow, *Sharing the Journey: Support Groups and America's
New Quest for Community* (New York: Free Press, 1994).

8. Taking so seriously the role of small groups, of course, in no
way negates the importance of large-group meetings. Both are essential
to healthy church life, as John P. Baker points out; see *Christ's Living
Body* (London: Cloverdale House, 1973), 39. On the one hand, he reminds us that churches that meet only as a large group run the risks of
remaining impersonal, inhibiting people from sharing their real needs
and joys, keeping members from growing, and preventing the emergence
of new leaders for the church's ministry. On the other hand, Christians
who meet only in small groups tend to be unaware of the needs and
responsibilities of the whole church, lack depth of understanding and
vision for the church's entire ministry and for gathering together for
worship and the sacraments.

9. Richard Halverson, "Fellowship: The Key to Witnessing," *His* 28, no. 3 (December 1967): 9-10.

10. Adapted from Leslie, *Sharing Groups in the Church,* 25, 33, 47, 138-163.

11. While Leslie suggests here that only some church members have a special interest in sharing with others at a personal level, I find, as I report in chapter 1, that the majority of church members desire to participate in a personal sharing group.

We must not overlook, however, the difficulty of developing trust, especially in small-town and rural churches. For trust to develop, we must risk self-disclosure; conversely, to risk personal sharing, trust must be present. When we fear that whatever we share with others will become known around town, it is simply too risky for us to share at a personal level. This problem was also dealt with in chapter 1.

12. This point is also made by Parker J. Palmer, "A Place Called Community," *Christian Century,* 16 March 1977, 253.

13. For empirical evidence supporting this point, see Thomas Kirkpatrick, "Conceptualizing and Measuring Relationship Satisfaction" (Paper delivered at the Western Speech Communication Association Convention, Phoenix, Arizona, 1978).

14. See Jack R. Gibb, "Defensive Communication," *Journal of Communication* 11, no. 3 (September 1961): 141-48.

15. Lyle Schaller has also discovered this phenomenon; see *Assimilating New Members* (Nashville: Abingdon, 1978), 112-113.

Schaller also points to Hartman's suggestion of developing group life according to our people's interests and expectations as a breakthrough given the declining interest in forming groups according to the traditional classifications of gender, age, or marital status; see Schaller's foreword to Warren Hartman, *Five Audiences: Identifying Groups in Your Church* (Nashville: Abingdon, 1989). Hartman suggests that group life can be formed around five distinct audiences that exist in most congregations: the fellowship group, the traditionalists, the study group, the social action group, and the multiple interest group.

C. Jeff Woods points out that the offer of diverse groups is an especially important motivational factor for involving people in small group activities; see *We've Never Done It Like This Before: 10 Creative Approaches to the Same Old Church Tasks* (Bethesda, Md.: The Alban Institute, 1994), esp. ch. 10.

16. Paul D. Hanson also makes this point; see *The People Called: The Growth of Community in the Bible* (San Francisco: Harper & Row, 1987), 499-518, 537-46. See also Julio R. Sabanes, "Biblical Understanding of Community," in *Man in Community: Christian Concern for the Human in Changing Society,* ed. Egbert De Vries (New York: Association, 1966). In the same volume James M. Gustafson discusses the importance of custom and tradition in the church to a sense of community; see "A Theology of Christian Community."

17. Celia A. Hahn discusses the connection between being in the church and in the world, reminding us that metaphors such as "servant" call the church to reach beyond itself; see *Growing in Authority, Relinquishing Control: A New Approach to Faithful Leadership* (Bethesda, Md.: The Alban Institute, 1994), esp. ch. 5-6.

18. C. Kirk Hadaway, Francis M. DuBose, and Stuart A. Wright also cite the crucial nature of such communication; see *Home Cell Groups and House Churches* (Nashville: Broadman, 1987), 139.

19. Adapted from Leslie, *Sharing Groups in the Church,* 25, 163-185.

20. Roy M. Oswald affirms the importance of a group facilitator and underscores the importance of training leaders to facilitate small groups; see *How to Build a Support System,* 98-100.

21. Leslie further develops this point in *Sharing Groups in the Church,* 136. Earlier in his chapter 6 (pp. 116-26), he wisely points out that sharing groups in the church are for normally functioning, healthy people and should not become therapy groups, substituting for the psychological services of a trained therapist.

Chapter 6

1. Other books in The Alban Institute's Church Leader's Core Library also view leaders as helpers: Celia A. Hahn, *Growing in Authority, Relinquishing Control: A New Approach to Faithful Leadership* (Bethesda, Md.: The Alban Institute, 1994) advises leaders to do what is needed to serve their groups rather than attempt to control things (see especially chs. 2 and 6). Gaylord Noyce, *Church Meetings That Work* (Bethesda, Md.: The Alban Institute, 1994), ch. 2, recommends that leaders help groups build effective consensus and exercise creative group action.

2. For additional ideas, see Noyce, *Church Meetings That Work,*

ch. 4. Noyce suggests specific skills to draw everyone into group discussion and particular roles to achieve participation by everyone.

3. Robert Leslie, *Sharing Groups in the Church* (Nashville: Abingdon, 1971), ch. 2.

4. Lyman Coleman, et al., *The NIV Serendipity Bible Study Book* (Grand Rapids: Zondervan, 1986).

5. For example, from volunteerism literature, both the Y.M.C.A. and the Girl Scouts publish extensive training handbooks on group leadership. See *Training Volunteer Leaders: A Handbook to Train Volunteers and Other Leaders of Program Groups* (New York: National Council of Young Men's Christian Association, 1974); and *Training-the-Trainer Resource Book* (New York: Girl Scouts of America, 1978). Likewise, the League of Women Voters publishes helpful training materials for leaders of discussion groups (see, for example, discussion-leader manuals from League offices in cities such as Los Angeles, Seattle, and Washington, D.C.). See also Harleigh Trecker and Audrey Trecker, *Working with Groups, Committees, and Communities* (Chicago: Association Press, 1979).

You can also recommend several fine comprehensive, theoretically based, practical small-group discussion leadership textbooks from the small group communication literature, including: Em Griffin, *Getting Together* (Downers Grove, Ill.: InterVarsity, 1982); Thomas Scheidel and Laura Crowell, *Discussing and Deciding* (New York: Macmillan, 1979); John Brilhart, *Effective Group Discussion* (Dubuque: Brown, 1986). See also Noyce, *Church Meetings That Work*.

Finally, publications of note from the religious community include Lindell Sawyers, *EQUIP (Experience in Questioning and Using Inquiry Procedures)*, (Philadelphia: Geneva Press, 1972), which follows the inductive method of group inquiry; Leonardo Boff, *Ecclesiogenesis: The Base Communities Reinvent the Church* (Maryknoll, N.Y.: Orbis, 1988), which is Latin America-based; Roberta Hestenes, *Using the Bible in Groups* (Philadelphia: Westminster, 1983), which offers a rich array of creative Bible study methods; Charles Olsen, *Cultivating Religious Growth Groups* (Philadelphia: Westminster, 1984); Walter Wink, *Transforming Bible Study: A Leader's Guide* (Nashville: Abingdon, 1989); Hans-Ruedi Weber, *Experiments with Bible Study* (Philadelphia: Westminster, 1981).

6. For additional information, see Rosalind Rinker, *Learning Conversational Prayer* (Collegeville, Minn.: Liturgical Press, 1992).

7. Leslie, *Sharing Groups in the Church,* 29-30. For further discussion, see Elizabeth O'Connor, *Journey Inward, Journey Outward* (New York: Harper & Row, 1968).

8. For further discussion of this point, see Gordon Cosby, *Handbook for Mission Groups* (Waco, Tex.: Word, 1975), esp. Part 1.

9. Richard Halverson, "Fellowship: The Key to Witnessing," *His* 28, no. 3 (December 1967): 9-10. I also referred to this article in summary in chapter 2.

10. Dennis Denning also speaks of evangelism overflowing from koinonia. See *We Are One in the Lord: Developing Caring Groups in the Church* (Nashville: Abingdon, 1982), 79. Likewise, writing from a British context, Amiel Osmaston also makes this point. See *Sharing the Life: Using Small Groups in the Church* (Bramcote, England: Grove Books, 1979), 7.

11. Cosby, *Handbook for Mission Groups,* 58-61.

12. For an excellent overall discussion of calling out people's gifts, see Hahn, *Growing in Authority,* ch. 6.

13. Clyde Reid, *Groups Alive—Church Alive* (New York: Harper & Row, 1969), 104.

Michael T. Dibbert and Frank B. Wichern, *Growth Groups: A Key to Christian Fellowship and Spirituality Maturity* (Grand Rapids: Zondervan, 1985), ch. 11, also recommend the direct approach and suggest that when group members simply describe the behavior of difficult members, desired change often occurs.

Likewise, Wayne E. Oates, *The Care of Troublesome People* (Bethesda, Md.: The Alban Institute, 1994), recommends an approach similar to Reid's for dealing with group members who are critical, judgmental, back biters, and power-seeking controllers. Oates suggests that groups express care for troublesome members by being gently direct and seeking to restore them to healthy participation. Rather than blaming these members, Oates believes groups share a responsibility to become part of their needed support system.

14. C. Jeff Woods, *We've Never Done It Like This Before: 10 Creative Approaches to the Same Old Church Tasks* (Bethesda, Md.: The Alban Institute, 1994), 37.

15. For further suggestions about managing conflict, see G. Douglass Lewis, *Resolving Church Conflicts* (San Francisco: Harper & Row, 1981).

Hahn, *Growing in Authority, Relinquishing Control,* ch. 5, uses the metaphor of the pastor as "coach" and demonstrates the value of taking a collaborative conflict management style.

Additional conflict management resources include: David Augsburger, *Caring Enough to Confront* (Ventura, Calif.: Regal, 1980) and Roger Fisher and William Ury, *Getting to Yes* (New York: Penguin, 1983).

Chapter 7

1. Results will, of course, vary. For example, after ten years of work in a Catholic parish, church renewal expert Arthur R. Baranowski found 25 percent of his members participating. He goes on to offer very helpful suggestions for involving the other 75 percent. See *Creating Small Faith Communities* (Cincinnati: St. Anthony Messenger Press, 1988), ch. 6.

Patrick J. Brennan, *Re-imagining the Parish* (New York: Crossroad, 1990), also finds that the process of generating small groups in Catholic parishes takes time; he urges continual interpretation: "A steady, continuous flow of information about and motivation for small groups would seem to be more of a need in the Catholic Church, where . . . our ecclesiology and . . . practice seem to have precluded the need for such things as small groups. It takes time to turn around a big ship," 57.

2. In all your promotional presentations, keep in mind the advice of C. Jeff Woods in *We've Never Done It Like This Before: 10 Creative Approaches to the Same Old Church Tasks* (Bethesda, Md.: The Alban Institute, 1994), esp. ch. 7: We motivate people more by their hearts than by their heads. It is not enough merely to announce program goals and list group purposes. Rather, we should describe opportunities in ways that touch people's hearts. Tell stories and give testimonials that tap people's felt needs and interests.

Appendix A

1. I include a more thorough discussion of leadership style in "Small Group Discussion Leadership in a Volunteer Organization: An Exploratory Investigation" (Ph.D. diss. University of Washington, 1981), 24-53, see also 2-20.

2. Celia Hahn, *Growing in Authority, Relinquishing Control: A New Approach to Faithful Leadership* (Bethesda, Md.: The Alban

Institute, 1994), ch. 2-3, also advises employment of a flexible leadership style. Hahn suggests that our people- or task-oriented leadership style depends on the context, that our leaders should do whatever they need to do in a particular situation. In short, our leaders need to draw on a repertoire of options so as to blend their own integrity with group demands.

Appendix B

1. I include a discussion of this instrument's development and validity in "Small Group Discussion Leadership in a Volunteer Organization: An Exploratory Investigation" (Ph.D. diss. University of Washington, 1981), ch. 3.

Appendix C

1. I report the development of this list of effective and ineffective leadership characteristics in "Small Group Discussion Leadership in a Volunteer Organization: An Exploratory Investigation" (Ph.D. diss. University of Washington, 1981), ch. 4.

Appendix D

1. Jack Gibb, "Defensive Communication," *Journal of Communication* 11, no. 3 (September 1961): 141-48.

2. See Thomas Kirkpatrick, "Conceptualizing and Developing Relationship Satisfaction" (Paper delivered at Western States Communication Association Convention, Phoenix, 1977).

3. See Ralph M. Stogdill, *Handbook of Leadership: A Survey of Theory and Research* (New York: The Free Press, 1974). In Stogdill's summary and discussion (see ch. 40, pp. 411-20), he points out that leaders should maintain a group's goal, direction, and role structure.

Appendix I

1. Underscore the importance of group members themselves determining the group's purpose and structure rather than allowing someone from outside to prescribe such agreements. Groups need a fairly loose rein so as to maximize their creativity and determine their own sense of direction. C. Jeff Woods includes a fine discussion of the importance of enhancing or balancing group stability *and* creativity in *We've Never Done It Like This Before: 10 Creative Approaches to the Same Old Church Tasks* (Bethesda, Md.: The Alban Institute, 1994), see esp. ch. 5.

BIBLIOGRAPHY

Augsburger, David. *Caring Enough to Confront.* Ventura, Calif.: Regal, 1980.

_____. *Caring Enough to Hear and Be Heard.* Ventura, Calif.: Regal, 1982.

Baker, John P., ed. *Christ's Living Body.* London: Cloverdale House, 1973.

Baranawski, Arthur R. *Creating Faith Communities: A Plan for Restructuring the Parish and Renewing Catholic Life.* Cincinnati: St. Anthony Messenger, 1988.

Boff, Leonardo. *Ecclesiogenesis: The Base Communities Reinvent the Church.* Translated by Robert R. Barr. Maryknoll, N.Y.: Orbis, 1986.

Bonhoeffer, Dietrich. *The Communion of Saints: A Dogmatic Inquiry into the Sociology of the Church.* Translated by R. Gregor Smith. New York: Harper & Row, 1963.

Brennan, Patrick J. *Re-Imagining the Parish: Base Communities, Adulthood, and Family Consciousness.* New York: Crossroad, 1990.

Brilhart, John K. *Effective Group Discussion.* Dubuque: Brown, 1986.

Callahan, Kennon L. *Twelve Keys to an Effective Church: Strategic Planning for Mission.* San Francisco: Harper & Row, 1983.

Campolo, Anthony. *Ideas for Social Action*. Grand Rapids: Zondervan, 1983.

Claypool, John R. *The Preaching Event*. Waco: Word, 1980.

Clemmons, William, and Harvey Nestor. *Growth through Groups*. Nashville: Broadman, 1974.

Clinebell, Howard J., Jr. *The People Dynamic: Changing Self and Society through Growth Groups*. New York: Harper & Row, 1972. Also published as *Growth Groups*. Nashville: Abingdon, 1977.

Coleman, Lyman, et al., eds. *The NIV Serendipity Bible Study Book*. Grand Rapids: Zondervan, 1986.

Committee on Social Witness Policy. *Keeping and Healing the Creation*. Louisville: Presbyterian Church (USA), 1989.

Cosby, Gordon. *Handbook for Mission Groups*. Waco: Word, 1975.

Denning, Dennis. *We Are One in the Lord: Developing Caring Groups in the Church*. Nashville: Abingdon, 1982.

Dibbert, Michael T., and Frank B. Wichern. *Growth Groups: A Key to Christian Fellowship and Spirituality Maturity*. Grand Rapids: Zondervan, 1985.

Fisher, Roger, and William Ury. *Getting to Yes: Negotiating Agreement without Giving In*. New York: Penguin, 1983.

Forest, James H. *Making Friends of Enemies: Reflections on the Teachings of Jesus*. New York: Crossroad, 1987.

Foster, Richard J. *Celebration of Discipline: The Path to Spiritual Growth*. San Francisco: Harper & Row, 1978.

Fromer, Paul. " Earth Movers and Fog Clouds." *His,* November 1968, 9-13.

Gerkin, Charles V. *Prophetic Pastoral Practice: A Christian Vision of Life Together*. Nashville: Abingdon, 1991.

Gibb, Jack R. "Defensive Communication." *Journal of Communication,* September 1961, 141-48.

Gilbert, Barbara G. *Who Ministers to Ministers? A Study of Support Systems for Clergy and Spouses*. Washington, D.C.: The Alban Institute, 1987.

Girl Scouts of the USA. *Training-the-Trainer Resource Book*. New York: Girl Scouts of the USA, 1978.

Griffin, Em. *Getting Together: A Guide for Good Groups*. Downers Grove, Ill.: InterVarsity, 1982.

Gustafson, James M. "A Theology of Christian Community?" In *Man in Community: Christian Concern for the Human in Changing Society*. Edited by Egbert De Vries. New York: Association, 1966.

Hadaway, C. Kirk, Francis M. DuBose., and Stuart A. Wright, *Home Cell Groups and House Churches*. Nashville: Broadman, 1987.

Hahn, Celia A. *Growing in Authority, Relinquishing Control: A New Approach to Faithful Leadership*. Bethesda, Md.: The Alban Institute, 1994.

Halverson, Richard. "Fellowship: The Key to Witnessing." *His,* December 1967, 9-10.

Hanson, Paul D. *The People Called: The Growth of Community in the Bible*. San Francisco: Harper & Row, 1987.

Hartman, Warren J. *Five Audiences: Identifying Groups in Your Church*. Nashville: Abingdon, 1987.

Hestenes, Roberta. *Using the Bible in Groups*. Philadelphia: Westminster, 1983.

Keyes, Ralph. *We, the Lonely People: Searching for Community.* New York: Harper & Row, 1973.

Kirkpatrick, Thomas G. "Conceptualizing and Developing Community in a Congregation." D.Min. Dissertation, San Francisco Theological Seminary, June 1978.

_____. "Conceptualizing and Measuring Relationship Satisfaction." Paper presented to the Western Speech Communication Association Convention, Phoenix, 1977.

_____. "Small Group Discussion Leadership in a Volunteer Organization: An Exploratory Investigation." Ph.D. Dissertation, University of Washington, 1981.

Kirschenbaum, Howard, and Barbara Glaser. *Developing Support Groups: A Manual for Facilitators and Participants.* La Jolla, Calif.: University Associates, 1978.

Kung, Hans. *The Church.* Garden City, N.Y.: Doubleday, 1976.

Kysar, Robert. *Called to Care: Biblical Images for Social Ministry.* Minneapolis: Fortress, 1991.

Leslie, Robert C. *Sharing Groups in the Church: An Invitation to Involvement.* Nashville: Abingdon, 1970.

Lewis, G. Douglass. *Resolving Church Conflicts: A Case Study Approach for Local Congregations.* San Francisco: Harper & Row, 1981.

Marcum, Walt. *Sharing Groups in Youth Ministry.* Nashville: Abingdon, 1991.

Miller, J. Keith. *A Hunger for Healing: The Twelve Steps as a Classic Model for Christian Spiritual Growth.* San Francisco: HarperSanFrancisco, 1991.

National Council of Young Men's Christian Association. *Training Volunteer Leaders: A Handbook to Train Volunteers and Other Leaders of Program Groups.* New York: National Board of Young Men's Christian Association, 1974.

Neusner, Jacob, ed. *Contemporary Judaic Fellowship in Theory and in Practice.* New York: Ktav, 1972.

Nisbet, Robert A. *The Sociological Tradition.* New York: Basic Books, 1966.

_____ *The Quest for Community: A Study of the Ethics of Order and Freedom.* New York: Oxford University, 1953.

Noyce, Gaylord. *Church Meetings That Work.* Bethesda, Md.: The Alban Institute, 1994.

Nyquist, James, and Kuhatschek, Jack. *Leading Bible Discussions.* Downers Grove, Ill.: InterVarsity, 1985.

Oates, Wayne E. *The Care of Troublesome People.* Bethesda, Md.: The Alban Institute, 1994.

O'Connor, Elizabeth. *Journey Inward, Journey Outward.* New York: Harper & Row, 1968.

Olsen, Charles M. *Cultivating Religious Growth Groups.* Philadelphia: Westminster, 1984.

Olsson, Karl. *Find Yourself in the Bible.* Minneapolis: Augsburg, 1974.

Osmaston, Amiel. *Sharing the Life: Using Small Groups in the Church.* Bramcote, England: Grove Books, 1979.

Oswald, Roy M. *Finding a Balance for Effective Ministry.* Washington, D.C.: The Alban Institute, 1991.

_____. *How to Build a Support System for Your Ministry.* Washington, D.C.: The Alban Institute, 1991.

Palmer, Parker J. "A Place Called Community." *Christian Century,* 16 March 1977, 252-56.

Peck, M. Scott. *The Different Drum: Community-Making and Peace.* New York: Simon & Schuster, 1987.

Potter, David, and Martin P. Anderson. *Discussion: A Guide to Effective Practice.* Belmont, Calif.: Wadsworth, 1963.

Prell, Riv-Ellen. *Prayer and Community: The Havurah in American Judaism.* Detroit: Wayne State University, 1989.

Reid, Clyde. *Celebrate the Temporary.* New York: Harper & Row, 1972.

_____. *Groups Alive—Church Alive: The Effective Use of Small Groups in the Local Church.* New York: Harper & Row, 1969.

Rice, Howard L. *Reformed Spirituality: An Introduction for Believers.* Louisville: Westminster/John Knox, 1991.

Rinker, Rosalind. *Learning Conversational Prayer.* Collegeville, Minn.: Liturgical Press, 1992.

Sabanes, Julio R. "Biblical Understanding of Community." In *Man in Community: Christian Concern for the Human in Changing Society.* Edited by Egbert De Vries. New York: Association, 1966.

Sarason, Seymour B. *The Psychological Sense of Community: Pros pects for a Community Psychology.* San Francisco: Jossey-Bass, 1974.

Sawyers, Lindell. *Equip: A Training Program for Leaders of Adult Discussions.* Philadelphia: Geneva, 1972.

Schaller, Lyle E. *Assimilating New Members.* Nashville: Abingdon, 1978.

_____. *Choices for Churches.* Nashville: Abingdon, 1990.

_____. "Looking at the Small Church: A Frame of Reference." *Christian Ministry,* 8, no. 4 (1977): 5-9.

Scheidel, Thomas M., and Laura Crowell. *Discussing and Deciding: A Desk Book for Group Leaders and Members.* New York: Macmillan, 1979.

Schulweis, Harold. "A Statement on the Havurah." *Raayonot* 3, no. 3 (Summer 1983): 2 9-32.

The Simple Living Collective—American Friends Service Committee. *Taking Charge: Personal and Political Change through Simple Living.* New York: Bantam, 1977.

Smith, Donald P. *Congregations Alive.* Philadelphia: Westminster, 1981.

Stogdill, Ralph M. *Handbook of Leadership: A Survey of Theory and Research.* New York: The Free Press, 1974.

Tournier, Paul. *Escape from Loneliness.* Translated by John S. Gilmour. Philadelphia: Westminster, 1962.

Trecker, Harleigh B., and Audrey R. Trecker. *Working with Groups, Committees and Communities.* Chicago: Association Press, 1979.

Valley Beth Shalom Havurah Packet. *Raayonot* 3, no. 3 (Summer 1983): 25-26.

Waskow, Arthur. *These Holy Sparks: The Rebirth of the Jewish People.* San Francisco: Harper & Row, 1983.

Watson, David Lowes. *Accountable Discipleship: Handbook for Covenant Discipleship Groups in the Congregation.* Nashville: Discipleship Resources, 1984.

Weber, Hans-Ruedi. *Experiments with Bible Study.* Philadelphia: Westminster, 1981.

Whitehead, Evelyn Eaton, and James D. Whitehead. *Community of Faith: Models and Strategies for Developing Christian Communities*. New York: Seabury, 1982.

Wiederkehr, Macrina. *A Tree Full of Angels: Seeing the Holy in the Ordinary*. New York: HarperCollins, 1990.

Wink, Walter. *Transforming Bible Study*. Nashville: Abingdon, 1989.

Woods, C. Jeff. *We've Never Done It Like This Before: 10 Creative Approaches to the Same Old Church Tasks*. Bethesda, Md.: The Alban Institute, 1994.

Wuthnow, Robert. *Sharing the Journey: Support Groups and America's New Quest for Community*. New York: The Free Press, 1994.

The Alban Institute:
an invitation to membership

The Alban Institute, begun in 1974, believes that the congregation is essential to the task of equipping the people of God to minister in the church and the world. A multi-denominational membership organization, the Institute provides on-site training, educational programs, consulting, research, and publishing for hundreds of churches across the country.

The Alban Institute invites you to be a member of this partnership of laity, clergy, and executives–a partnership that brings together people who are raising important questions about congregational life and people who are trying new solutions, making new discoveries, finding a new way of getting clear about the task of ministry. The Institute exists to provide you with the kinds of information and resources you need to support your ministries.

Join us now and enjoy these benefits:

CONGREGATIONS: The Alban Journal, a highly respected journal published six times a year, to keep you up to date on current issues and trends.

Inside Information, Alban's quarterly newsletter, keeps you informed about research and other happenings around Alban. Available to members only.

Publications Discounts:

☐ 15% for Individual, Retired Clergy, and Seminarian Members
☐ 25% for Congregational Members
☐ 40% for Judicatory and Seminary Executive Members

Discounts on Training and Education Events

Write our Membership Department at the address below or call us at 1-800-486-1318 or 301-718-4407 for more information about how to join The Alban Institute's growing membership, particularly about Congregational Membership in which 12 designated persons receive all benefits of membership.

 The Alban Institute, Inc.
Suite 433 North
4550 Montgomery Avenue
Bethesda, MD 20814-3341